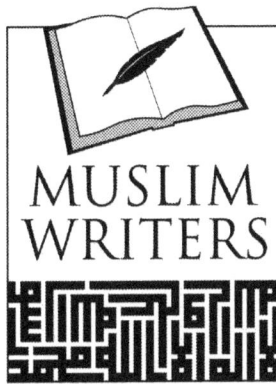

MUSLIM
WRITERS

Praise for the *Islamic Rose Books* Series

"Folks, you have to check this one out. *Islamic Rose Books* are fun, wholesome and educational. We need more Islamic fiction titles like these as alternatives to the uninspiring literature some of our children are reading these days. Personally, I'm hooked to the books. I think even adults, especially those who are new to or clueless about Islam, will benefit from reading them. Great way to do da'wah as well, so you can get them for your children's non-Muslim friends or even yours! The stories read naturally, especially the conversations. I hope your books will do well and will certainly tell others about them."

- Salinah Aliman, Author, Singapore

"I was pleasantly surprised to come across the *Islamic Rose Books* series by Sr. Delgado, a convert to Islam and accomplished and dedicated author. It wasn't just one well-written book, however, but four, so our eager young readers can continue to grow and experience life with the main character of the series, a young girl named Rose and her non-Muslim friends group called the Hijab-Ez, who take us on a journey of self-discovery as well as the discovery of Islam. We are presented with a number of very serious life moments and through engaging story-telling we are brought to realistic resolutions. The writing is terse, though not sparse, free-flowing, but not shallow. I, personally, plan to introduce these books in our Islamic school and also to donate them to our local library. Definitely recommend for your book shelves!"

- Yahiya Emerick, Author and Educator:
What Islam Is All About

"Linda D. Delgado, a retired police-woman, offers a unique introduction to Islam, Muslim life and Islamic practices through her four Rose books for children. Each book revolves around 9-year-old Rose's first meeting with Muslims from overseas. The books, designed as family entertainment, include recipes, poetry, interesting facts about places, and a glossary of Islamic terms. These books will be a welcome addition to school libraries."

- Islamic Horizons Magazine - Review

"I'm so happy to finally read a book to my children that shows that being different, no matter if its your age, color of your skin, religion or the language you speak.....we can learn to accept each other and deal with every day issues in a way that God would approve. My children loved the silly adventures Rose gets herself into and the way she always tries to do the right thing. We are a Christian Family and found the books to be a first step in showing that ALL people can get along no matter what your beliefs are. All we have to do is CARE for each other! I'm glad we read the books and look forward to the other books in this series!"

- Ramona Vazquez
Miami, Florida, USA

Also by Linda D. Delgado

Islamic Rose Books Series

The Visitors (Book One)
Hijab-Ez Friends (Book Two)
Stories (Book Three)
Saying Goodbye (Book Four)

Non-fiction

Halal Food, Fun and Laughter
A Muslim's Guide to Publishing and Marketing

Stories

Linda D. Delgado

Muslim Writers Publishing

Tempe, Arizona

Stories

Muslim Writers Publishing
P.O. Box 27362
Tempe, Arizona 85285
USA

www.MuslimWritersPublishing.com
and www.widad-lld.com

Library of Congress Catalog Number: 2005935794

ISBN 978-0-9767861-7-7
ISBN 0-9767861-7-6

Illustrations by Shirley Angum Gavin
Book cover designed by Zoltan Rac-Sabo
Interior design by A.P. Fuchs

Printed in the United States of America

Special Thanks

Special Thanks and love to my husband of thirty-one years, Raymond Delgado, a good cop, husband, father and grandfather.

Special Thanks to police officers Abdulraham AH Alwaily and Fahd Khalf Al-Harbi, from Riyadh, Kingdom of Saudi Arabia.

Special Thanks to Debora McNichol for her encouragement and support of my work.

Special Thanks to my friend and copyeditor, Pamela K. Taylor.

Special Thanks to my dear friend, Judy Nelson-Eldawy, for giving me permission to use the poems she wrote specifically for my books.

A Very Special Thanks to my dearest friend and author, Amatullah Al-Marwani.

**Bismillah Ar-Rahman, Ar-Raheem
In the Name of Allah,
Most Gracious, Most Merciful**

Dedication

Islamic Rose Books would not have been written without the Help of Allah and then the help, imagination and inspiration of my dear granddaughter, Cassy A. Tedla (my Islamic Rose).

Stories

Table of Contents

Introduction — *Islamic Rose* Family and Friends

Rose—Leader of Hijab-Ez, ten-year-old only child, Christian background, mixed ethnicity, USA.

Camelia—Member of Hijab-Ez, ten-year-old only child, Muslim, Egyptian-American, USA.

Ruby—Member of Hijab-Ez, eleven-year-old only child, Protestant Christian, Vietnamese National

Christina—Member of Hijab-Ez, ten-year-old with four siblings, Catholic Christian, Hispanic-American, USA.

Grandma (Linda)—Rose's grandma, police officer, avid gardener, loves crafts, searching for truth about God, doesn't claim any religious affiliation, believes in God but not the Trinity, mixed ethnicity, USA.

Grandpa (Ray)—Rose's grandpa, retired police officer, works evenings in security, Catholic Christian, Hispanic-American, USA.

Dad (Tony)—Rose's father, single parent, lives next door to Rose's grandparents, Catholic Christian, mixed ethnicity, USA.

Fahd—Saudi Arabian police officer, lives at Grandma's home for one year, Muslim, kind and smiles a lot, great story teller

Abdul—Saudi Arabian police officer, lives at Grandma's home for one year, Muslim, loves books and astronomy

Sylvia—Grandma and Rose's friend, owner of The Phoenician Restaurant, married to an Arab Muslim, mixed ethnicity, USA.

Judy—Camelia's mother, Muslim revert born in USA, loves jewelry, co-owner of Casa Camelia Restaurant, married to an Egyptian, USA.

Kendall—Rose's six-year-old cousin, Hispanic-American, Catholic Christian parents, USA.

Definition: Hijab-Ez (pronounced 'hijab-ease') is a word Rose made up to identify the group of Muslim and non-Muslim friends who joined together to support her hijab-wearing school friend, Camelia. A member of the Hijab-Ez is a girl who wears a head covering regardless of her religious beliefs.

Prologue

Fahd and Abdul are Saudi Arabian police officers who came to the USA for one year and are staying at Grandma's house. They have successfully completed a six-month English course and have begun six months of police academy training. They have been sharing their culture and Islamic values with Rose, her family, and her friends.

Ten-year-old Rose and her three friends are known at their public school as the Hijab-Ez because Rose, Ruby, and Christina wear headscarves each day to school to support their friend Camelia, who is a Muslim. During the first semester of their fifth grade year, the four girls have become loyal friends. They have met and overcome many challenges, and their friendship has been tested. The diversity of their religious beliefs and ethnic backgrounds has united the four girls not divided them. During the second semester of the school year, the Hijab-Ez will face many new challenges at school and with their families. The wisdom in the Islamic stories they hear from Fahd and Abdul and life-experience stories from family members may help them overcome problems and make good decisions.

❧

Christina noticed Camelia twisting the paper and asked, "Why are you twisting that paper, Camelia? It looks like you are trying to be a human

Linda D. Delgado

shredding machine!" No one laughed at Christina's attempt to lighten the mood around the table with her little joke.

Ruby couldn't stand it anymore. She grabbed the crumpled paper from Camelia and began smoothing out the wrinkles. Christina thought, "Oh boy! There is something seriously wrong happening here! Camelia didn't protest when Ruby grabbed the paper from her hands."

Rose suddenly slammed her hands down on the table and muttered loudly, *"It's not fair!*

"What's not fair?" Christina squeaked nervously as she looked at a now angry-faced Rose.

"I'm so mad I could bite nails!" Ruby nearly shouted in an angry voice. Her three friends looked at Ruby with shocked expressions on their faces. Ruby almost never raised her voice and never, ever got mad!

"Shish," whispered Camelia. *"Everyone is looking at us!"*

Ruby's face reddened and she whispered back, *"Well, Rose is right. It's not fair!"*

1

Three Special Stories

Rose burst into the family room where Grandma, Fahd, and Abdul were sitting and talking about next week's firearms training assignment. "It's not fair! They are just being mean! I don't want to go to that Sunday school class ever again!" Rose nearly shouted as she flung herself into Grandpa's recliner and began to bawl like a newborn baby.

Grandma, Fahd, and Abdul were momentarily shocked into silence. Rose had ridden to her Sunday school class with their neighbors, Mr. and Mrs. Gleason. When she left, she was cheerful and smiling, even though Grandpa could not take her today because he had to go to work.

Grandma seemed to recover first. She went to Rose and said calmly, "Rose, please calm down and tell us what has happened. We can't help you if we don't know what the problem is."

Through her sobs, Rose recounted what had happened that morning. "The boys and girls are going on an overnight camping trip, and mothers are going with the girls, and fathers with the boys. They are going to visit Colossal Cave Park. The boys are going one day, and the girls are going another day. I can't go because I don't have a mom to go with me. I asked if it was okay for my dad to come with me, and the teacher said no!"

"Can I go with you, Rose?" Grandma asked.

"The teacher suggested I bring my grandmother, but I told her my dad is also my mom and he should be the one to come with me. She said she was sorry, but my dad couldn't go with me. None of the other girls is having a grandma go with them. Then that girl, Mary Higgins, made fun of me and said I must be an orphan. The other kids laughed and asked me why I didn't have a mom. One kid even asked if my mom was dead! I didn't know what to say to them. Even the teacher asked me where my mother was!"

"Maybe they were just curious or trying to be helpful?" Grandma suggested.

"I think they were just nosey, and, if they wanted to help me, why did some of the kids laugh? Most of the kids already know I don't have a mom. They treat me different, like they never ask me to go to their houses after class or anything. I know when somebody is making fun of me, Grandma."

Fahd and Abdul looked at Rose with concern mirrored on their faces, but waited to see what Grandma would say to Rose.

"If you really want to go on this trip, I think I can get off work and go with you." Grandma offered again.

"I don't want to go if my dad can't go. What I don't understand is why they called me an orphan. Besides, being an orphan doesn't make a person bad, does it?" Rose questioned.

"Of course it doesn't, and you are not an orphan. You have your dad who loves you very much," replied Grandma in her no nonsense tone of voice.

Grandma handed Rose a Kleenex and suggested, "Why not go wash your face. It will make you feel a little better, and then we can talk some more."

Rose nodded her head and left the family room to do as Grandma suggested. While Rose was temporarily away from the family room, Grandma quickly explained to Fahd and Abdul why Rose was so upset.

"But, Mum, Rose is not an orphan. She has her father, you, and her grandfather. It was most unkind for the other children to laugh at Rose," Fahd said disapprovingly. Grandma could tell he was upset because Rose's feelings had been hurt.

Abdul said carefully, "I do not know what to say to Rose about this class. I think we should try to make her not feel so sad. Fahd, you like to tell stories, and Rose loves to hear them. You must tell her your story about the 'Unlettered Man.' He was indeed an orphan, but grew up to be a great trader in Arabia, and later Allah chose him to be the Last Prophet."

A look of relief crossed Grandma's face as she nodded her head and smiled at Abdul. "That is an excellent suggestion. Thank you, Abdul."

Fahd nodded his head in agreement just as Rose walked back into the family room. Rose gave everyone a wan smile as she settled back into Grandpa's recliner and gave a big sigh.

Fahd smiled at Rose and said, "Remember when I promised I would tell you a story about one of the greatest traders in Saudi Arabia? It was right before the day of the bazaar, when you and your Hijab-Ez friends sold your crafts to raise money for the new Islamic school."

Rose's ears perked up when she heard the word "story." She straightened up in her chair and turned her attention to Fahd. Rose nodded her head, pushed her long bangs from her face, and said in a quavering voice, "I remember."

"This great trader was an orphan!" Fahd said dramatically. "Would you like for me to tell you how he became an orphan and then grew up to be the great trader? I call this great trader 'the Unlettered Man.'"

Rose was hooked. Gone were the sighs and frowns. Rose's sad expression changed to one of animation, and she replied with enthusiasm, "I want to hear the story, Fahd."

Thank goodness. I think the worst of the storm is over! Grandma thought as she watched Rose's attention move beyond the morning's events and focus on listening to Fahd's story.

Fahd began his story with, "The Story of the Unlettered Man. About one thousand five hundred years ago in the Arabian lands lived a tribe called…"

Abdul interrupted, "Wait, Fahd. I think you should start the story before this; maybe start with the family background of this great trader."

Fahd frowned at Abdul. He hated when anyone interrupted his storytelling, except for Rose and his little sister back home in Saudi Arabia. "That will make the story very long," Fahd argued good-naturedly.

"Rose won't get to hear about the Cloud Miracle or about the miracle of the lost ZamZam Well being found," countered Abdul. Abdul could be just a little stubborn at times.

"Oh, I want to hear about the miracles, too!" exclaimed Rose.

Fahd looked at Rose's face. Her eyes were gleaming with excitement. "I would not want to disappoint our young Rose, so I will begin again."

Rose clapped her hands, and Grandma gave her "that look." Rose quickly folded her hands in her lap and pretended to zip her lips closed.

Fahd cleared his throat and began again. "A couple of thousand years have passed since Allah gave the ZamZam Well to Hajar and Isma'il. Many Arabs are now traveling to Mecca to put wooden and stone idols in the Ka'bah that Prophet Abraham and Isma'il built to thank Allah. The people hardly remember Allah. The ZamZam Well is covered over and no one knows where it is. They have to bring fresh water to the city of Mecca by camel.

"There was a man named *Abdul Muttalib* living in Mecca. He was very poor and belonged to the *Banu Hashim* clan of the *Quraish* tribe. He hadn't forgotten Allah and he spent his time digging all over the city of Mecca looking for the ZamZam Well. One day, he said a prayer to Allah and asked for help to find the well. Abdul promised if Allah helped him and also gave him ten sons, he would sacrifice one of his sons in thanks.

"Allah guided him to the place of the ZamZam Well, and, in time, Abdul had ten sons. His youngest son was named *Abdullah*, and everyone loved him. Abdul knew he had to keep his promise to Allah, but was very unhappy, as he did not want to sacrifice Abdullah. Many of the people heard about Abdul's oath to Allah, and they suggested he go see an old woman for advice. She told him to write the words 'Abdullah' and 'ten camels' on lots (like a piece of paper) and put the lots in a container. Abdel drew

Abdullah's name ten times before he finally drew the lot with the words 'ten camels.' The old woman told Abdul this meant he was to sacrifice one hundred camels to Allah. Abdul was very happy and thanked Allah for not requiring him to sacrifice his son.

"Abdullah grew up and was known to be a good and honest man. When he was twenty years old, he married Aminah, who was from the *Banu Zahra* clan that lived in Mecca. Abdullah decided to go on a business trip to *Ash-Sham*, which means Syria. Aminah did not want him to leave her because she was going to have a baby. Abdullah brought Aminah an African servant woman named *Barakah* to help her while he was away on his trip.

"A terrible tragedy happened to Abdullah. On his way home he got very sick and died. Aminah was very sad, but her father-in-law, Abdul Muttalib, took care of Aminah after his son died. One night, before her baby was born, Aminah had a dream and heard a voice tell her to name her baby Muhammad when he was born. Muhammad means 'Highly Praised.' When Aminah had her baby boy it was the year 570."

"Oh, Fahd," cried Rose with tears in her eyes. "The poor little baby doesn't have a father!" Grandma looked a little teary-eyed, too. Fahd quickly told Rose not to worry because the story would have many happy parts.

"When Muhammad was six years old, he and his mother traveled to the city of *Yathrib*, which is known today as *Medina*. Muhammad's father was buried in Yathrib, and Aminah wanted to visit his grave. Every day, his mother went to the grave and cried so much that she became ill. When they traveled back home, she got sick and knew she would die very soon. Aminah asked her friend and servant, Barakah, to promise to love and care for young Muhammad. Barakah promised and said she would never leave Muhammad."

Rose gasped when she heard this. "Poor little boy! Now he doesn't have a mom or a dad!"

Grandma patted Rose's knee and reached for a Kleenex. "Please don't interrupt Fahd again, Rose," Grandma quietly pleaded. Rose nodded her head and accepted a Kleenex from Grandma.

Fahd nodded to Grandma and continued with the story. "Poor Barakah! She had to dig the grave and bury Muhammad's mother before she and Muhammad returned to the grandfather with the sad news. Now little Muhammad was an orphan."

"This story is so sad," said Rose. "Does it get better for little Muhammad?"

"You are perhaps sad because you also lost your mother, young Rose?" said Abdul.

"Yes, but I still have my dad," Rose murmured through her sniffles. Abdul smiled encouragingly to Rose, and she smiled back.

Fahd continued, "Muhammad lived with his grandfather for four years, and then his grandfather became ill and died. Barakah and Muhammad went to live with his uncle, *Abu Talib*. Abu Talib had already promised the grandfather he would raise Muhammad as though he were his own son.

"When Muhammad was twelve years old, his uncle decided to go on a business trip to Syria. His uncle was a trader and decided to take many camels on the trip. Muhammad asked to go with his uncle. After Muhammad had asked several times, his uncle finally agreed. Muhammad was given the job of taking care of the camels each evening when the caravan rested.

"After traveling about two weeks, the caravan approached a small town. Just outside this town was a Christian monastery where a monk named *Bahira* lived. Bahira noticed a dark cloud following above and providing shade for the caravan."

"I know what is special about the cloud!" said Rose in an excited voice.

"So, Little Sister, what is so special about this dark cloud?" inquired Abdul.

"God put the cloud there," said Rose with a big grin.

"Our Little Rose is very wise," said Fahd. "It is true. Allah has caused clouds to make constant shade over every Prophet." Rose nodded her head as if she already knew this.

Fahd continued, "Bahira wanted to meet everyone in the caravan, so he invited them to have supper with him. Bahira looked at everyone and was disappointed. He knew someone was missing. He asked Abu Talib if there was anyone else in his caravan, and Abu Talib sent for Muhammad. When Bahira saw Muhammad, he was excited, happy, and spent all evening talking to Muhammad. He later told Abu Talib that Muhammad was the Last Prophet chosen by Allah, and Muhammad was a very special person!"

"Wow!" The word just slipped out of Rose's mouth before she could stop it. She clamped her hand over her mouth and looked sheepishly at Grandma. "Sorry."

Fahd waited a moment after Rose's unusual comment before continuing with his story. "When Muhammad was a teenager, he went to a meeting at the house of a man named *Abdullah ibn Jud'an*. The people at the meeting wanted to form a charity to help care for all the poor in Mecca. At the meeting, the people made a special pledge promising to help the poor and needy, assist the oppressed, protect the weak, secure the rights of people, and help establish peace and harmony among people. Muhammad made this pledge and he practiced it all his life. When he grew to be a young man, many people began calling him *As-Sadiq*, which means 'Truthful One.'

"As a young man, Muhammad worked for his uncle as a shepherd and he spent many nights gazing at the stars and moon in the sky. He wondered about Allah and decided he didn't believe that the idols were gods. He saw people make the idols with their own hands. Instead Muhammad wanted to know more about Allah."

Fahd paused to clear his throat, and Abdul took the opportunity to ask Rose, "Did you know that every Prophet has been a shepherd when he was a young man or boy?"

"No, I didn't know that, but I know Prophet David was a shepherd."

Fahd looked sternly at Abdul and sighed in exasperation at another interruption. "No more talking or I will never finish my story!"

Abdul and Rose traded small smiles and then said contritely to Fahd, "Sorry."

"Now back to my story. Muhammad never had the opportunity to go to school so he didn't know how to read or write. This is why I called him 'the Unlettered Man.' Back in the days of Arabia, most people did not go to school. They did not have schools like we have today in Saudi Arabia and like you have in your country, Rose.

"As Muhammad grew older, he decided to learn to be a trader. His uncle gave him some items for trading, and Muhammad took them to the bazaar in the city. He liked seeing all the different people and wonderful goods that came from far away places. He was a good trader and earned the reputation of being kind, fair, and well mannered. He never cheated anyone and he always made a profit. People began to call him *Al-Ameen*, which means 'The Trustworthy'."

Fahd paused and heard Abdul whisper to Rose, "You and the Hijab-Ez are good traders."

"We had so much fun at the masjid bazaar. I hope we can make crafts to sell at the next one," Rose whispered back.

Grandma, who had been very quiet and attentive while listening to Fahd, suddenly said, "I think the Muslims at Camelia's masjid will be very happy if the Hijab-Ez help again. All of your profits were donated to help build the new Islamic school."

Fahd smiled and thought to himself, *Telling stories here in this country is very different from telling stories with my family, but Rose is so eager to learn, and I don't really mind when she interrupts me!* "I think I will finish my story another time. Maybe Rose and Grandma have some other things they want to do?" Fahd said teasingly.

"Please, please, finish the story Fahd," pleaded Rose. "I want to find out what Muhammad does next."

Grandma laughed and said, "Maybe Fahd will finish his story if all of us stop interrupting him!"

Abdul laughed and said, "Fahd would tell stories all day and all night. He is just teasing you, Little Sister."

Fahd grinned at Rose and once again resumed his story. "When Muhammad was about twenty-five years old, he wanted to marry, but he was too poor. His uncle, Abu Talib, wanted to help him so Abu Talib went to visit a very rich widow named Khadijah. She owned many caravans. Abu Talib persuaded her to allow Muhammad to be the leader of her next caravan. Khadijah promised she would pay Muhammad very well if he did a good job.

"Khadijah didn't know Muhammad, so she had her trusted servant, *Maysara*, go with the caravan to watch Muhammad. Muhammad went to many towns and sold all the items for very good prices. The servant was very impressed at how fair and honest Muhammad was in his dealings with people.

"When all the trading was finished, Muhammad began the journey back to Mecca. Maysara suggested that Muhammad ride ahead and make a report to Khadijah on how well the caravan had done. This would permit Khadijah the chance to meet Muhammad.

"Khadijah met with Muhammad and decided she liked and admired him because he was honest and he had excellent manners. Days after this meeting, she began to miss him and she told a friend, *Nafisa*, she would like to marry Muhammad. She was forty years old and a widow, and Muhammad was only twenty-five years old, so she thought he would not want to marry her.

"Nafisa decided to tell Muhammad about Khadijah wanting to marry him and her worries he wouldn't want to marry her because she was older and a widow.

"Muhammad listened to Nafisa and said he was too poor to get married. Nafisa asked him, 'If money did not matter would you want to marry Khadijah?' Muhammad said he would. For the next three months, Khadijah and Muhammad thought about getting married to each other and finally decided to get married. They were very happy in their marriage."

Fahd paused momentarily and then said, "I am going to stop my story here, Little Sister. It is getting late, and your dad will want you home soon. Another time, I will finish my story. I will tell you how Muhammad was called by Allah to tell others about Islam."

"You won't forget to finish your story will you?" asked Rose.

"No, Little Rose, I will not forget," said Fahd.

"This story is about a real orphan, but he still had extended family to take care of him and help him," Grandma said to Rose.

"Yes…he had his grandfather and then his uncle and the friend of his mother, who always stayed with him, too!" Rose added. "I like this story."

"Remember, he grew up to be very successful as a trader and he found a very good wife. This tells us that orphans are good people and can have happy lives," Abdul added.

Rose nodded her head and smiled at her two older Saudi brothers.

As if on cue, the telephone rang, and Grandma went to answer it. She returned to the family room and said to Rose, "Your dad just got home from work and he wants you to go home. Do you want me to talk to him about the field trip and what happened at Sunday school today?"

"Thanks, Grandma, but I think I will tell him what happened. I need to ask him some questions about my mom," replied Rose.

Rose hugged Grandma, Fahd, and Abdul, and thanked Fahd for his story before leaving for home.

❧

"Dad, I'm home," Rose called out as she walked through the kitchen of the house.

"I'm in the sunroom," Dad called back.

Rose walked slowly down the hallway towards the guest bedroom, which led to the sunroom. Dad called it the sunroom because it was added to the house after the house was originally built. All three walls and the double doors leading out to the backyard were made of windows. Dad had blinds installed to provide shade from the bright Arizona sun.

Rose loved the hallway. Dad had hung framed pictures of Rose since she was a baby on the walls. The framed photographs lined both sides of the hall. Rose often laughed at some of the pictures showing her doing silly things. One of her favorite pictures was when she was a baby sitting in a highchair with

Grandpa trying to feed her oatmeal. Grandma took the picture when Rose spit the oatmeal out, and it landed on Grandpa's face!

"How was your day?" Dad asked with a smile for his best girl.

"It started off pretty good, and then I got upset and mad at Sunday school. I told Grandma about everything, and Fahd told me a story about an orphan and trader, and now I don't feel so bad. I'm still a little mad because it isn't fair!" Rose said in a rush.

"Whoa! Why don't we go sit in the living room and you can explain everything to me?" Dad suggested as he hugged Rose.

Rose nodded and followed her dad to the living room. Rose and her dad sat down on the green, over-stuffed couch, and dad clicked off the television. "Now that we are comfortable, begin with why you are upset, tell me what isn't fair, and then you can tell me why you are still a little mad," Dad suggested.

Rose explained what had happened at Sunday school, and, as she finished, she gave a deep sigh. "Dad, I think I was upset with those kids because I didn't know what to say about my mom. We never talk about her and why she left. I can't tell people she's dead, because I don't know anything about where she is or why she left us."

Rose's dad looked at his daughter's troubled expression and sighed. "I had hoped I wouldn't have to talk to you about this for a few more years, Rose. I don't have the answers you are looking for. I can tell you what I do know and what I think. Okay?"

Rose nodded and looked steadily at her dad.

"After you were born, your mother was depressed. The doctor said this was normal for many new mothers because they have to go through many physical and emotional adjustments. Your mom returned to work, but was unhappy all the time. She said she didn't want to quit work, so I didn't know what to do about her unhappiness. When you were about six months old, I came home from work and found the apartment where we were living completely empty. Everything was gone. The neighbor across from us came out of her apartment holding you and your diaper bag. She told me your mother asked her to watch you while we moved to a new apartment. Your mother never returned for you. She didn't leave me a note and she never called."

Rose gulped, but said bravely, "Did you see her at work and ask her why she left and took everything?"

"Rose, your mom quit her job and did not tell anyone at her job what her plans were or where she was going. They were as surprised as I was."

Brushing at the silent tears in her eyes, Rose asked softly, "What did you do, Dad? Did you try to find my mom?"

"Yes, I did. I contacted her sister, but she had not heard from your mom. I went to the police, but I was told your mom left of her own free will and there was nothing they could do about it."

"Her sister?!" Rose practically shrieked. "You never told me my mom had a sister! You never told me you knew any of my mom's relatives!" Rose said in a slightly accusing tone of voice.

"I'm sorry, Rose. You never asked me any questions about your mom before. I guess I was just waiting until you did ask," Rose's dad said.

Dad seemed to be uncomfortable saying this. At least, that is what Rose thought. *I'll ask him about my aunt later. Right now I want to know about my mom.*

"Were you mad at my mom?"

"Yes, Rose. I was hurt and mad. I didn't know what else to do. I went to your grandma and grandpa, and told them what had happened. They invited me to move into their house for a short time, until we could get this house next door to them. Grandpa retired and began taking care of you because Grandma wasn't close to retirement time and I needed to work to support us. We went to see a judge, and he gave me custody of you. Your mom did not come to the court to see the judge."

"But, did she know about the judge?" Rose persisted, hoping her mom maybe didn't know about the judge.

"Yes, she did. The police finally found her living in Tucson, and gave her papers telling her about the hearing with the judge. I guess she decided not to come to the hearing. Your Grandma found her in Tucson and tried to convince her to get some help for the problems she was having. Grandma paid for your mom to go to a treatment center. Your mom went to the treatment center, but only stayed two weeks. One day, she just walked away and didn't return. We haven't heard anything from her since then."

Rose said, with sad tears rolling down her cheeks, "I am very sad for my mom, but I'm mad at her, too. She didn't even think about me."

"I'm sad for her, too, Rose, and I was mad for a very long time. I had to stop being mad, because being mad made me feel sick, and it was keeping me from being happy about having you," Dad replied heavily and gave Rose a hug. Dad waited patiently while Rose fought to control her tears. Finally, she sighed deeply and used the Kleenex her Dad handed her to blow her nose and dry the remaining tears from her eyes.

"I don't think I want to tell those kids or the teacher about my mom. What should I say if people ask me about her?"

"Why not just say the truth? Your mom left when you were a baby, and you don't know why, or where she is," suggested Dad.

"Okay. I'm not an orphan, either, because I have you!" Rose said with a hint of defiance.

"You have Grandma and Grandpa, your aunts, uncles, and cousins, too. You have lots of family, Rose, and we all love you very much."

"Fahd told me a story about a real orphan. His dad died, and then his mom. He lived with his grandpa, until his grandpa died when he was only ten years old. Then the boy—his name is Muhammad—went to live with his uncle until he grew up. Even if he was an orphan, he still had lots of family to take care of him. Just like me!" Rose said and smiled for the first time since the conversation began.

"Fahd was very kind to tell you a story that helped you feel a little better."

"Dad, you know what I noticed about Fahd and Abdul? They never seem to get mad, and they don't say angry words about people when I tell them about things that upset me."

Rose's watched as a look of surprise flickered across her dad's face. "Dad, Fahd and Abdul always tell me a story when I get upset. I think it is their way to help me understand and think about things that bother me!"

"When I was a young boy and had problems, I would tell Grandma and she would do the same thing. She never really told me what to do. She would tell me a story that helped me to think about things, and often I would learn a lot from the story."

"Please tell me one of the stories about when you were a boy and had a problem," Rose pleaded.

Dad scratched his head and thought for a few moments while Rose waited expectantly.

"When I was ten or eleven years old, I loved baseball and wanted to be a famous baseball player. I heard about a new baseball team being started for kids my age and I wanted to join the team. Your grandma was concerned about me having a problem playing baseball because, back then, I had to wear glasses. My glasses had black frames, and the lenses were very, very thick. I used to have a lazy eye." Before Rose could ask what a lazy eye was, her dad help up his hand to stop Rose's question.

"A lazy eye is when one or both of your eyes have weak muscles. Your eyes turn inward when you try to focus on things. I had one lazy eye and had to wear the glasses that your grandma and the eye doctor said would make my eye stronger."

"Oh, I understand now," Rose said nodding her head.

"Grandma explained to me that trying to focus on the baseball when I was up to bat might be hard to do. I wanted to play baseball so much that I didn't listen to Grandma. I tried out for the team and got accepted because every kid got accepted. I did a good job in the outfield, but after we started playing other teams, I started having problems. Every time I took my turn at bat, I would strike out. I would try to focus on the ball, but I couldn't see it right. Pretty soon, the other boys on the team started calling me four-eyes and making fun of me at practice when I practiced extra hard at batting the ball."

Rose's face changed from a sad look to an indignant look as she listened to her dad. "What happened, Dad? Did you get into a fight?"

Rose's dad chuckled. "Yes, I did. I got into so many fights that the coach told me I would not get to be on the team if I didn't stop fighting. He called your grandma and told her I was a big problem for the team because I hadn't learned how to get along with other kids."

"But...didn't you tell the coach about the boys' name calling and stuff?" Rose sputtered.

"Nope, I was so mad and I liked to fight them."

Rose's eyes seemed to grow larger with astonishment at hearing her dad say he wanted to fight. "Did you get in trouble with Grandma?" Rose asked, having concern for the little boy her dad once was.

"Nope, I didn't and was I surprised. Grandma and I had a talk. She explained that one day I wouldn't need to wear my glasses any more, and, if I was patient, I might find another sport to play. She said I had a choice: I could return to the baseball team and not fight, or I could quit and find another sport I might like to do. She said if I quit that would be okay and if I stayed with the team that would be okay."

Rose was really enjoying the story and could hardly wait to find out what happened next. "What did you decide?"

"First, I told Grandma that I couldn't decide. That's when she told me a story that helped me make a decision. Grandma said that when she was a little girl, she would spend summers and weekends with her grandpa. Once, she got some flower seeds in the mail and wanted to plant them. It was wintertime, and the ground was very hard, and in many places still covered with snow. Her grandpa explained to her that it was not the right time to plant seeds. The weather conditions would cause the seeds to grow into weak plants, and they probably wouldn't survive the cold. Her grandpa told her that if she was patient and waited until the right time, in the spring, she could plant the seeds with his help. With patience and care, the seeds would become beautiful flowers. Grandma said her grandpa cautioned her. He told her that by the time spring came, she might decide that she didn't want to plant flowers in her garden. She might decide that she wanted to plant vegetables."

Rose had an uncertain look on her face and asked with a slight hesitation, "Did you understand Grandma's story?"

Dad chuckled when he heard Rose's question and saw her face. "I guess you could say that I thought your grandma just didn't understand. Her story didn't seem to make much sense to me. I think I must have looked just like you do right now!"

"Did Grandma explain the story about planting seeds?" Rose asked hopefully.

"Yes, she did. She said the seeds were like my eyes. The seeds were weak and would not do well planted in the winter. My eyes were weak and would not allow me to do well right then playing baseball. If I was patient until my eyes grew stronger, I could one day play baseball. Just like her being patient and waiting for the right time to plant her seeds in the spring."

"But...what did her grandpa mean about Grandma changing her mind and choosing to plant vegetables instead of flowers?" Rose was very curious about this part of the story.

"Grandma explained that I might find another sport I liked better, if I decided to quit playing baseball. She said maybe not right away, but if I was patient, an opportunity might just be around the corner!"

"So, Grandma said you might play baseball when your eye got strong, or maybe you might want to play a different sport?" Rose asked.

"Yep, and she was right. I quit the baseball team. When school started, I tried out for the football team and played the tackle position all through high school."

"And...your eye was all well, and you didn't need those ugly glasses!" Rose ended her dad's story and smiled.

"I wish," Dad laughed. "I wore those ugly glasses until I was in the eleventh grade and I still ended up in a fight now and then because some kid would call me four-eyes. I didn't need to focus in on the football, playing a tackle position on the team. Having a weak eye didn't matter when playing football."

Rose and her dad both laughed when he finished his story.

"I like learning from stories," Rose said and smiled.

"I think we still have to talk about the field trip. I can talk to your Sunday school teacher about the trip, or maybe you might want to reconsider and ask your grandma to go with you? It sounds like a fun trip. I've never been to the Colossal Caves. You might even find some cool rocks for your collection," Dad suggested.

Rose didn't answer her dad right away.

Dad waited patiently for Rose, who appeared to be thinking hard about their discussion.

After a few moments, Rose answered. "I would really like to go to the Colossal Caves, but not with the Sunday school group. I know I have to get used to not having a mom to go with me to different things, but I still get sad. If you could go, I wouldn't be so sad. It's sometimes hard to see the kids at school with their moms and especially on holidays like Mother's Day. No, Dad. I don't want to go camping with the group. Maybe our family can go see the cave sometime," Rose asked hopefully.

"Are you sure, Rose?" Dad asked softly.

"Yes, I am sure. I'll tell Grandma and Grandpa tomorrow morning. If I don't, my grandpa will be hopping mad and go argue with the Sunday school teacher!" Rose said and grinned just thinking about her grandpa yelling at the Sunday school teacher.

"I think you are right about Grandpa!" Dad said and chuckled.

"Did you eat supper at your grandma's house?" Dad asked.

"No, and I am sooo hungry, now!" Rose exclaimed.

"Let's order a cheese pizza and watch a John Wayne western. How does that sound?"

"Yum," Rose said and hugged her Dad good and hard. She felt like a big weight had been lifted from her heart.

2

Caves

The next morning, Rose sat in the dining room at Grandma's house eating the eggs and toast Grandpa had made for her breakfast. Grandma had left for work before Rose came over from her house to get ready for school. Grandpa was his cheerful self and hadn't mentioned anything about what had happened at Sunday school yesterday. Rose decided to ask him if Grandma had told him anything.

"Did Grandma tell you about the field trip my Sunday school class is planning and they won't let my dad go with me?"

"Yes, she did. Your dad called last night, too, probably after you went to bed, and we had a long talk. I have been thinking about everything. Ever since you left the Christian school, you have not had good experiences with the kids you used to go to school with. These are mostly the same kids in your Sunday school class, right?"

Rose nodded her head and took another bite of toast.

"Your dad, Grandma, and I think we should begin going to another church. The one at the end of our street is always sending us invitations to attend a church service. Would you like to go there next Sunday?"

"Super!" Rose nodded her head vigorously, jumped up, ran to her grandpa, and hugged him.

"You know that changing where we go to church will not stop new people we meet from asking about your mother?"

"I know that. But, now, I am going to say the truth and not worry about what other people think. I don't have any answers, so they will just have to accept what I say," Rose replied with a hint of defiance.

"Good for you, Rose. Now finish your breakfast. I have to brush your hair and listen to all your ouches and squeals! School starts in fifteen minutes. We better get moving and don't forget to brush your teeth! Your grandma told me to remind you."

Rose grinned and headed for the bathroom and her waiting toothbrush.

❧

The Hijab-Ez sat at their usual end of the table in the lunchroom. Camelia was telling them about the bird that her cat, Mouser, had dragged into the restaurant dining room causing a big uproar from her dad and one of the waitresses.

Rose was only half listening. She was trying to decide if she should tell her friends about what happened yesterday. *They all have moms, so maybe they won't understand. Maybe I should just tell them Fahd's story,* Rose mused.

When Rose didn't laugh at the conclusion of Camelia's funny story, her friends noticed she was preoccupied. "Earth to Rose! Earth to Rose!" Christina said loudly to get Rose's attention.

Rose looked at the three curious faces of her friends. *May as well tell them and see what they think,* she thought.

"I was thinking about yesterday." Rose explained what had happened, her discussion with her dad, and the family decision to change churches. "So, what do you think?" Rose asked.

Camelia was the first to speak up. "This Sunday school class has some of the same girls that are in that Girls Club you went to?"

Rose nodded her head.

"You never told us anything, but I always thought something happened when you went to that meeting with your old school friend. I think your family is making a good decision to change where you go to church."

"I agree with Camelia," Ruby said in her usual, soft voice. "I don't know why they were so rude by asking you all those questions about your mom. Lots of kids don't have moms, or dads, and some kids are being raised by their grandparents!"

"That's right," Christina added. "My cousin's dad left after the divorce and he's been gone for ten years. He never calls, writes, or visits my cousin, Andrea. It's not the kids' fault parents do these things!"

"You probably get sad on days like Mother's Day and stuff, but you have a super grandpa and grandma!" Camelia offered to comfort her friend.

"The only thing I'd miss about the whole deal is seeing Colossal Cave," Christina said.

"Christina, keep your mind on the discussion," Camelia gently chided.

Christina made a silly face at Camelia and all four girls laughed.

"Thanks for understanding. I feel better just talking to all of you," Rose said and smiled at her good friends.

"Hijab-Ez! Friends forever!" Camelia said as she raised her pinkie finger in the air. Ruby, Rose, and Christina echoed Camelia's friendship call.

❧

Sunday dawned bright and early for Rose. The sun was just beginning to peek over the horizon when Rose's alarm clock buzzed. Rose opened her sleepy eyes and pushed the tangled mass of hair off her face. As she stretched, she remembered that today was Colossal Cave Day! Rose, Grandma, Grandpa, Fahd, and Abdul were driving to the Colossal Cave Mountain Park to explore the Cave, visit the museum, and have a picnic. It had been Dad's suggestion that the family go there this weekend, and everybody had agreed. The fun day ahead was only marred by the fact that Rose's dad wasn't going with them.

I wish Dad was going with us, thought Rose as she quickly got dressed. Dad had been called in to work last night, and Rose had spent the night at her grandma's house.

"Good morning, Grandma and Grandpa. As-Salaam'-Alaykum, Fahd and Abdul." Everyone was sitting around the dining room table eating breakfast when Rose greeted them with smiles and hugs.

"Wa'alaykum as-Salaam, Rose," greeted Fahd and Abdul.

Grandma smiled at Rose and said, "We have everything packed and are ready to leave after you finish your breakfast."

"How long will it take us to get there?" asked Rose.

"About two hours." Grandpa set aside his morning newspaper and planted a kiss on top of Rose's head.

Rose looked at Grandpa and asked, "Can I ride with Abdul and Fahd?"

"Yes, if you eat all your breakfast. We won't be stopping on the way and we won't be eating again until lunch time," Grandma reminded Rose as she went to the kitchen to finish cleaning the dishes and putting food away in cupboards and the refrigerator.

Rose finished her breakfast and hurried out the back door to feed her cat friends. Cappy wanted to play, but Rose mildly scolded him, "Not today, Cappy. I'm in a hurry. We are going to visit the Colossal Cave today, and I have to put my backpack, note pad, and pencils in Abdul's car."

Rose hurried into the house, gathered her backpack, and followed Fahd to the car. Abdul and Grandpa were talking about the directions to Colossal Cave. Rose heard Abdul tell Grandpa, "We will follow you."

Once they were traveling south towards the Colossal Cave Mountain Park, Rose pulled out her notepad. "Do you want to hear what I learned about the Colossal Cave?" asked Rose.

"I think Rose did some research on the computer," Fahd teased.

"Yes, I did. I'll read my notes to you and Abdul."

"The Colossal Cave is owned by and located in Pima County, Arizona, which is in southeastern Arizona. The cave goes inside a mountain for five miles. It was first used by the Hohokam

Indians around 900 AD. From about 1456 to 1880, the Sobaipuri Indians used the cave for shelter, too. In 1879, a pioneer named Solomon Lick discovered the entrance to the cave.

"Ah...let's see...umm... in 1905, a seventy-five-foot tunnel was made so a mining company could gather bat guano (waste). Bat guano is used to make gunpowder. In 1923, guided tours of the cave were offered to visitors. Early pioneers built the *La Posta Quenado*. La Posta Quenado means 'burned post office.' During the early pioneer days, a stagecoach would stop at this ranch and bring mail. Local Indians, like the Apache and Papago, didn't like all the settlers moving onto their lands. I think the Indians must have fought the miners!

"By 1992, the Mountain Park around Colossal Cave had grown to over two thousand acres. The park is full of Saguaro cacti. Southeastern Arizona is the only place where this cactus grows naturally, and it takes one hundred years for a Saguaro to grow one arm from the main body of it. The park has lots of coyotes, which the Indians call Song Dogs because they howl a lot every night.

"Okay...I'm looking for how big it is. Here it says that the cave is six hundred feet into the mountain and starts forty feet below the entrance that was made bigger so people could tour the cave. The cave is dry now and has a constant temperature of about 70 to 71 degrees. The cave was formed ten to fifteen million years ago, and the stalactites and stalagmites were formed long ago when the cave was wet." Rose finished reading her notes and looked up at Fahd, who was sitting in the front seat of the car across from Abdul.

"That was very interesting. Thank you for this information," said Abdul. Fahd nodded his head at Rose.

"I'm going to make a report on the Colossal Cave for school. Do you think I have enough information?"

"I think you did a good job researching about the cave. Once we get to the park, you might find some more information at the museum," replied Abdul.

Rose nodded her head and replied, "That's a good idea."

"Fahd, do you know any Islamic stories about caves? Do you have caves in Saudi Arabia?"

"We have many caves in Saudi Arabia. There is a special cave that I am thinking of right now. It is very famous because Prophet Muhammad (peace and blessings be upon him) had miracles happen to him in this cave." Fahd just had to smile when he saw Rose's eyes widen at the word "miracles."

"Miracles! Please tell me about the cave!" sputtered a very excited Rose. Fahd's stories always made Rose's eyes shine, and when miracles were added to a story...*well, this just has to make the story extra special*, she thought.

Fahd began to tell his story. "Today, I will tell you about the Cave of *Hira*. After Muhammad got married, he had time to think about many things. I told you that he didn't believe in praying to idols that were made by men. He didn't like the way the poor people were treated by the town's people. He was troubled and restless. He often took walks out into the hills and countryside around Mecca to think about Allah. He wanted to know about Allah and since he never learned to read or write, all he could do was think about the world and creations Allah made.

"He heard about a small cave in a mountain, and one Monday, he decided to go to the cave to have some quiet time. It was such a good place to think that soon he began going to this cave often.

"In the year 610, when Muhammad (pbuh) was forty years old, he took another walk to the Cave of Hira. The cave was often damp and cold. He sat there thinking, and suddenly the cave seemed to fill with light and grow very warm! The light was so bright that he was dazed. Then he heard a loud voice say, 'Read!' The voice sounded like it was coming from everywhere inside the cave. He was very scared and all he could answer was, 'I can't read.' Then his chest felt like it was being squeezed very tight and the voice told him again, 'Read!' Muhammad (pbuh) said again, 'But, I can't read.' A third time the voice said, 'Read!' Finally, Muhammad (pbuh) couldn't stand the squeezing of his chest anymore and he said, 'What should I read?'"

Linda D. Delgado

"I would be very scared," whispered Rose with a voice filled
with awe and wonder as a small shiver ran up and down her
spine.

Fahd continued with his story. "Then, the voice stopped.
Muhammad (pbuh) was so scared he rushed out of the cave and
ran down the mountain trail to get home. Suddenly, the voice
came from the sky all around him! The voice said, 'Muhammad,
you are the Messenger of Allah and I am Jibra'il (Angel Gabriel).'
Muhammad (pbuh) saw a vision of a man filling the whole sky.
Muhammad (pbuh) ran even faster now. He didn't understand
what was happening. When he got home, he was shaking with
fear and told his wife, Khadijah, to cover him. She held him until
he fell into an uneasy sleep.

"After Muhammad (pbuh) fell asleep, his wife went to find
some help for her husband. She went to her wise, blind cousin,
Waraqa, and asked him for advice. Her cousin was very excited
when he heard what Muhammad told Khadijah. Waraqa told her
that the voice was the same voice that talked to Prophet Moses.
This meant that Muhammad had been chosen by Allah to be a
Prophet.

"When Khadijah returned to check on Muhammad, she saw
him sleeping, but he was mumbling words and he was sweating.
His words sounded like poetry! When Khadijah woke
Muhammad, he told her, 'Khadijah, the time for resting is over.
Jibra'il has asked me to warn people and call them to Allah and to
His service. But who shall I call?'

"Khadijah smiled and said she would accept Muhammad's
call and she became the first person to accept Islam."

"Do you like this story?" asked Fahd.

Rose nodded her head. "You mentioned this cave before in
another story, but you didn't tell me everything. What happens
next to Prophet Muhammad?"

"Many, many things happen, Little Rose, but today I will
finish my story by telling you just a little about the first believers
in Islam."

"Okay, but can I ask just one more question, please?"

"What is it that you want to know?"

"Did Muhammad ever go back to the cave?"

"Yes, after he understood what Allah wanted him to do, he wasn't afraid anymore. Now, I will finish my story and NO more questions!" smiled Fahd.

"Not long after this, the messages from Angel Gabriel stopped. Muhammad got very sad. He missed the messages and the beautiful words that sounded like poetry. He thought maybe he had done something wrong, and perhaps Allah was angry with him. After about six months, the Prophet heard Angel Gabriel again. This time Angel Gabriel taught Prophet Muhammad (pbuh) how to make Wudu' and Salah. He also taught him the first surah, Al-Fatihah."

"Excuse me, Fahd, but how long did it take for Prophet Muhammad to receive all the information that is in the Qur'an?" questioned Rose.

"Prophet Muhammad received the Qur'an during twenty-three years from the time Angel Gabriel first told him to READ," answered Fahd.

Abdul interrupted and said, "Let me explain a few things to you, Rose, so you will understand what was happening at this time in history. During those twenty-three years, the Prophet (pbuh) was busy teaching the new believers in Islam how to live differently. The new believers became known as Muslims when they decided to serve Allah. They had to make many changes in their lives. The Prophet (pbuh) taught them how to make wudu' and pray five times a day. Allah wants Muslims to have clean bodies and minds, so the Prophet (pbuh) had to teach the people how to take proper baths, clean their teeth, and eat foods that were good for their bodies.

"The new Muslims belonged to tribes, and each tribe had a leader. Now, the new Muslims wouldn't follow these tribal leaders anymore, but followed the teachings of Islam, which are to serve Allah first. Prophet Muhammad (pbuh) taught them to free slaves, treat their wives and daughters kindly, and have good manners towards family and neighbors."

"So they didn't follow the tribal way of living anymore?" asked Rose.

"That is right. This made many leaders mad at the Prophet (pbuh), and they began to be afraid of him, too, because the people would no longer listen to the tribal leaders or worship idols." Fahd and Abdul both smiled at Rose. They were happy Rose understood how Islam first began to grow in Arabia.

"I think the Prophet had a big job to try and convince the people about Allah. Probably some of them didn't want to change and give up their idols. Maybe they were scared to try and change." Rose gazed thoughtfully out the car window for a few moments.

Rose had another question, "Who else became a Muslim after Khadijah?"

Abdul looked at Fahd, and Fahd answered Rose. "The second Muslim was a man named *Zayd ibn Harith*. Zayd had been a slave, but Prophet Muhammad (pbuh) freed him. He became like a son to the Prophet (pbuh) and Zayd never left him. The next person was the nine-year-old nephew of the Prophet (pbuh). His name was *Ali*. Prophet Muhammad (pbuh) had a very good friend named *Abu Bakr ibn Abi Quhafa*. He was very well known, wealthy, and the head of his clan. Abu Bakr knew and trusted the Prophet. When he heard what the Prophet said about there being only one God, Allah, and how people must change and treat others with kindness and respect, Abu Bakr also became a Muslim."

"How many new Muslims do we have now, Little Rose?"

"We have 1-Khadijah, 2-Zayd, 3-Ali, and 4-Abu Bakr," Rose counted out loud, raising a finger on her right hand for each new Muslim.

"You are right. There is one more important new Muslim," said Abdul. "Do you remember the woman who helped raise Muhammad after his mother died? Remember the woman who promised never to leave Muhammad?"

Fahd and Abdul waited while Rose pretended to put on a thinking cap. She muttered a few words under her breath. "I don't know if I will say the name right, but I think the new Muslim was the woman called Barah?"

"You are right! Her name in your English is spelled Barakah," offered Fahd in a kind and encouraging voice.

Rose's smile seemed to shine and light up her face. She loved being right!

"Now, I will finish my story," said Fahd as he grinned back at Rose. "For the next couple of years, Prophet Muhammad (pbuh) told only people he knew and trusted about Islam. His daughters, and many close friends, and relatives believed what the Prophet told them and they became Muslim. The Prophet did not go out and speak at public meetings, or bazaars and such, at first. He had a good idea that the tribal leaders would not like what he had to tell them. He spent his time teaching the first believers so they would be strong in belief and be able to help him in later years."

"That was a really good story, Fahd. Look!" Rose pointed to a road sign that said "Colossal Cave Mountain Park, 2 Miles."

"We're almost there, and it's a good thing because I'm getting hungry again!"

Fahd reached into his backpack, took out a bag of grapes, and handed them to Rose. "Maybe this will help your tummy stop growling like a mountain lion." Fahd and Abdul laughed as Rose popped a juicy purple grape into her opened mouth.

They arrived at the park well before noon and went to find a picnic location. Grandpa had arranged by telephone with the Park Service people for Rose and her family to tour the cave at 2:00 PM. This gave them plenty of time to eat lunch, visit the Park Museum, and for Fahd and Abdul to say Dhuhr prayer.

Rose eagerly took her rock-collecting bag from her backpack and began searching the ground for some special rocks to take home. Soon, Fahd, Abdul, Grandma, and Grandpa were busy looking for special rocks for Rose, too.

Fahd and Abdul got out the cameras Grandma had given them and began taking pictures of the desert and mountain landscape. The Saguaro cacti were everywhere and some had pink and yellow blossoms on them. Some were very tall, reaching over twelve feet or more. Grandpa and Rose continued to rock hunt, while Grandma, Fahd, and Abdul toured the museum.

꩜

After they finished their tour of the cave, Grandma noticed Rose was very quiet. "Is something wrong or troubling you, Rose? Didn't you enjoy visiting the cave?"

"It was lots of fun, but I thought the cave would be bigger. Remember when we watched that Explorer TV show about the cave? I remember it being bigger and deeper. This cave was dry and the one on the Explorer show was a cave that had water in it making it damp and kind of cold."

"You are thinking about the show we watched that described the Carlsbad Caverns in New Mexico. The Carlsbad Caverns are much larger and have recently had a lot of work done on tunnels for disabled visitors access," replied Grandma.

"Oh, well, that explains why I got confused," smiled Rose.

"Did you have a good time?" asked Grandpa as they began loading his car with the picnic supplies and gift shop items Grandma had bought at the museum.

"Yes! Thank you, Grandma and Grandpa. It was super fun, and I found some awesome rocks for my collection. I can't wait to get home so I can wash them and look at them with my magnifier. When we were driving here, Fahd told me another story. It was about a cave in Arabia, miracles, and how the Muslims got the Qur'an!"

"Well, I want to hear all about this cave in Arabia and the miracles!" Grandma hugged Rose and smiled at her Saudi boys.

"I think I will ride home with you and Grandpa so I can tell Fahd's cave story," exclaimed Rose.

Rose climbed into the back seat of Grandpa's car and waved to Fahd and Abdul as they drove away from the parking lot towards the park gate. *Oh, Fudge! I should have made some notes while Fahd was telling me the cave story. Now I'll have to write them when I get home,* she muttered silently. Rose settled back in the seat and blinked her eyes. Suddenly, she felt tired and sleepy. "Grandma, I think I'll just rest my eyes a few minutes," Rose said sleepily.

Grandma and Grandpa looked back and smiled. Rose was already fast asleep. Grandma and Grandpa were going to have to wait for another time to hear Fahd's special cave story.

❧

Rose saw her friends waiting by the wall for her, waving frantically. She gave Grandpa a quick hug and hurried down the walkway. *What's up with the Hijab-Ez? I can't wait to tell them about the Colossal Cave and Fahd's story about Angel Gabriel appearing to Muhammad,* Rose thought as she quickened her pace.

"Hijab-Ez!" Rose greeted her friends and they yelled back, "Hijab-Ez!"

Before Rose could get two words said, Christina grabbed Rose's arm and pulled her closer. Ruby and Camelia huddled with the two girls. "Hey, what's going on?" Rose said expectantly as she looked at her three friends.

"You are not, I mean N-O-T, going to believe this!" Christina whispered dramatically.

Rose waited and waited, and still her three friends just looked at her. "Will somebody puh-lease tell me what I won't believe?"

"Ruby overheard it in the Library this morning when the teachers were meeting, and then Camelia saw a note Mrs. Rodriguez dropped in the hallway, and the note said right at the top, 'District Three Board of Supervisors Approval' and under that it said…" Christina paused and grinned at Rose. Rose's eyes were squinting, like they do when she really concentrates.

Rose could hardly contain her curiosity. "Christina! If you don't tell me right now, I promise you I won't…I won't speak to you the rest of the day!" Rose sputtered.

"The note said that school is approved for Saturday!" Christina finished in a hushed voice.

"Are you telling me that we are going to have to start going to school on Saturdays?" Rose squealed.

Ruby, Christina, and Camelia looked at Rose solemnly and nodded their heads.

"It's true," Camelia said. "I saw the note with my own eyes!"

Rose looked at Ruby. Ruby always was so calm and never got too excited about stuff. "Ruby, just what did you overhear in the library?"

Camelia looked at Rose crossly and spoke up before Ruby could answer, "I know what I saw and read, Rose."

"I'm sorry, Camelia. I didn't mean to sound like I didn't believe you," Rose said contritely.

Camelia smiled at Rose and looked over at Ruby.

"The teachers were having a short meeting this morning in the library. I got here early so I could help the librarian put the new books we got Friday on the shelves. I heard the principal ask the teachers if they thought the parents would agree to us kids coming to school on Saturday. I didn't hear the rest because I had to go to the other end of the library where the new books needed to be put on shelves," Ruby said matter-of-factly.

"I sure don't wanna go to school on Saturdays!" Christina said vehemently. The rest of the Hijab-Ez echoed Christina with, "Me, either!"

"The school has to tell our parents. Maybe the teacher will give us a flyer to take home today?" Camelia offered.

"Something this big…I think the principal might send a letter in the mail," Ruby offered.

"I'm gonna tell my dad and grandparents that I think they should protest this. It's not fair to us kids," Rose exclaimed.

"My mom and dad won't like it and they will protest because they'll have to find a babysitter for my two sisters if I'm at school on Saturdays," Christina said confidently.

The first bell rang for class, and the Hijab-Ez decided to see what else they could find out about having to go to school on Saturdays before they said anything to anyone else.

3

Meteorite Crater

Grandma sat in her car waiting for the school day to end. It was 3:15 PM, and the last bell would ring in five minutes. Grandma had a busy day at work and thought she was going to be late to pick up Rose from school. *Five minutes to spare!* Grandma sighed in relief.

She rolled down the car window and thought, *spring is coming early this year to the Arizona desert.* The early mornings and evenings were still cold, but the afternoons were getting warm. Already, many of the fruit trees and flowers had blossoms. The green summer grass was edging up through the brown winter grass. The wild flowers were erupting along the roadways and throughout the desert, and the cacti showed signs of blooming soon.

In just a few short months, Fahd and Abdul would complete their police training, and then they would return to their homes in Saudi Arabia. Grandma didn't like to think about the day they would leave. The past year had been such a wonderful experience–getting to know the young men and learn about their lives, their customs, and Islam. *Rose will have a hard time saying good-bye.* "Me, too," Grandma said out loud.

Grandma looked across the road and saw Rose waving to her. School was over for the day, and Rose was walking very fast towards the car. Grandma smiled and wondered what news Rose had to tell her. Every time Rose walked fast from the classroom, Grandma knew she was excited. When Rose walked very slowly, trouble was usually brewing.

"Grandma, Grandma!" exclaimed Rose. "Guess what?"

"The sky is falling? You have been chosen to receive one hundred cats? A visitor from Mars arrived at your school today?" teased Grandma.

"Oh, silly Grandma, we are going on a field trip to the Meteorite Crater!" Rose exclaimed excitedly.

"When do we leave?" Grandma quipped. Rose made a funny face at Grandma.

"Our class is going, and Grandpa can come as a teacher assistant, too! We are going next Saturday! Here is the permission sheet, and it tells all about the trip. Dad won't want me to miss this trip!" Rose nodded her head vigorously and grinned widely, showing the gap on the upper right side of her mouth where she had recently lost one of those annoying baby teeth.

"Want to hear something really funny?" Rose asked and grinned impishly at Grandma.

Before Grandma could say yea or nay, Rose continued. "When I got to school this morning, Ruby said she overheard the principal talking about parents approving students going to school on Saturdays, and then Camelia read the top part of a note Mrs. Rodriguez dropped in the hallway that said the school board had approved students going to school on Saturdays." Rose stopped to see Grandma's reaction. She was disappointed.

"Really?" Grandma said mildly.

"Well, anyways, when I got to school, the Hijab-Ez told me about this, and we all thought this meant we were going to start going to school *every* Saturday! It's a good thing we decided not to say anything to any of the other kids! Boy, would we have looked silly. The note and the principal were talking about the field trip for this Saturday!" Rose finished her funny tale.

"I bet you and the Hijab-Ez spent the whole day plotting, scheming, and trying to find out more information," Grandma teased Rose, and her eyes twinkled as she began to chuckle.

Rose began to laugh and said, "It is kinda funny, isn't it? I sure am glad we were wrong!"

"Well, it's a good thing you didn't tell anyone else. Do you know what this kind of story is called? It's a story that is only partially true, but misleads people?"

"A rumor?" Rose ventured.

"Yes, a rumor. Some rumors can hurt people and get people in trouble. Young people and older people often get caught up in rumors. The more a rumor gets told, the more untrue it becomes," Grandma said with a more serious tone of voice.

"We didn't spread it around, so we didn't get into any problems. We sure learned a lesson today. Now that it is all over, it seems funny, but it wasn't funny all day. When the teacher gave us the flyers about the field trip, I was sooo relieved!"

"I think all the Hijab-Ez were relieved," Grandma said with a smile for Rose.

Rose nodded and went back to reading the flyer.

"Grandma, did you know that a meteorite is a huge rock? The crater is where it landed when it fell from space. It got so hot that most of it burnt up before it hit the ground. It ..." Rose suddenly stopped talking. She hadn't paused between sentences and now she needed to gulp some air and catch her breath.

"My, aren't you excited. I'm sure Grandpa is going to love going on the field trip with you. You can ask Grandpa to sign the teacher assistant form when you see him in the morning. I'll read the flyer when we get to the house." Grandma smiled at Rose and helped her fasten the seat belt.

In just a few minutes, Grandma and Rose arrived home. Rose's school was only six blocks from home. Rose lived in a large city, and it wasn't safe for kids to walk on the streets by themselves. When Rose first saw the new public school, she asked if she could ride her bicycle to school. Grandma's warnings quickly put an end to Rose's short-lived bicycle plan. Grandpa used to have to drive her all the way across town in heavy traffic just to get to her old school in the mornings. She had to get up an hour earlier in the mornings last year.

Rose got out of the car and went to the back gate. She was going to visit with her three cat friends: Midnight (because she was all black), Taffy (because he pulled on things and stretched all the time), and Cappy (because he had a black spot on the top of his head that looked like the outline of a baseball cap). The cats mewed and rubbed against Rose's pant legs. "Hello, my friends! Did you miss me? Did you have fun today?" Rose asked her cat friends as she scratched their ears.

Rose sat down in the middle of the glider and began pushing it back and forth with her feet. Midnight jumped onto her lap, and Cappy and Taffy jumped on to the glider seat for a ride, too. Rose told her cat friends about the field trip. "I'm going to search the whole crater and find the best rocks ever," she confided to her cat friends.

"I need my rock collecting bag!" Rose jumped up suddenly and the cats jumped after her. Rose went to the outside laundry room door. Glancing back, she saw the three cats sitting in an attentive row, each gazing up at her expectantly. "No, I am not getting you any snacks. I am going to look for my rock-collecting bag." Rose opened the door and went to the shelves Grandpa had saved for Rose to store her outdoor playthings.

"Rose, where are you? You forgot your book bag in the car. You have homework and piano practice to do before your dad gets home from work," Grandma called to Rose from the backdoor opening.

Rose didn't answer Grandma. Grandma looked out the back door, but didn't see Rose. Grandma was exasperated and yelled loudly, "Rose!"

"I'm in the laundry room looking for my rock collecting bag," Rose answered as she poked her head out the laundry room doorway.

"You have a whole week to find it. Right now you need to do your homework."

"Okay, I'm coming," Rose called back. Rose wiped her dusty hands on her pants and closed the laundry door behind her. Her cat friends looked at her expectantly. "Surprise!" giggled Rose as she gave each of her friends a cat snack.

Rose walked back to the front patio. As she opened the car door to retrieve her book bag, she heard Grandma calling her again. "What is the rush?" Rose wondered aloud. "I'm coming. I'm coming," yelled Rose. She hurried through the front door and saw Grandma standing at her desk holding out the telephone receiver.

"Ruby wants to talk to you. She says it is real important," explained Grandma as she handed the telephone to Rose.

Ruby was the quiet Hijab-Ez. When she talked, Rose, Camelia, and Christina shut up and listened. Ruby had a very soft voice, and, when she used it, she usually had something important to say. *It must be really important for her to call me*, Rose thought.

Ruby's favorite hobby was making animals and shapes from colored paper. She carefully creased the paper, and then, with a series of complex folds, her wonderful animals, flowers, and geometric shapes began to appear as if out of nowhere! Ruby then used her art supplies (watercolors, markers and even glitter) to decorate her art projects. Her beautiful decorations could be seen fluttering from strings all around her bedroom. Ruby and Rose both loved animals and Ruby very generously had given Rose many decorated paper animals. During "Save Our Animals Week," Ruby and Rose collected money from neighbors to donate the money to the local animal shelter.

Rose picked up the telephone receiver and said, "Hello, Ruby, long time, no see!" Rose giggled.

"My mom doesn't want me to go on the field trip," Ruby near-whispered sadly, "even though I told her your grandpa would look after me since he was going on the trip, too."

"I haven't asked my grandpa, yet. He's at work and I won't see him until morning," said Rose.

"Oh, no!" wailed Ruby.

"Are you okay?!" exclaimed Rose. She had never heard Ruby raise her voice. *This is serious*, Rose thought. "Calm down! Calm down, Ruby! I am sure he will be going. He loves to go on my field trips. I'll ask my grandma to talk to your mom, okay?"

"Okay, I'll get my mom," Ruby said a little more calmly.

Rose went into the kitchen where Grandma was brewing some tea and explained Ruby's problem. Grandma happily agreed to talk to Ruby's mother.

Rose waited anxiously beside Grandma as she talked to Ruby's mother. After a few minutes, Grandma handed Rose the telephone. "Everything is okay for Ruby. Her mother has agreed to allow her to go on the field trip," Grandma said and then she hugged Rose.

"Feel better now?" asked Rose.

"Please thank your grandma for me. I am sooo happy!" replied Ruby in an unusually animated tone of voice.

"See you at school tomorrow. I have to get my homework done and practice my piano. Grandma has already reminded me twice. The third time and my dad will hear about it!" Rose raised her voice when she spoke this last sentence. She was hoping Grandma would overhear what she just said to Ruby about her lessons and piano practice.

"See you tomorrow," said Ruby as Rose hung up the telephone.

"Will Fahd and Abdul be coming home early today?" Rose asked her Grandma.

"No, dear, they are going to the barbershop for a haircut after Maghrib prayer. They have an inspection tomorrow. They are going to Mohamed's apartment after they have their haircut to get their uniform, weapons, and boots clean and ready," Grandma replied.

"Why don't they do all that here at home? Then I could see them more often," Rose halfheartedly pouted.

"Mohamed's wife is cooking lamb and rice for supper. You know I can't cook lamb right, and lamb and rice is the boys' favorite," said Grandma.

"If you were fixing my favorite food, I wouldn't go anywhere else to eat, either," said Rose. She grinned at Grandma to let her know she wasn't going to pout anymore.

"Fahd and Abdul told me that as soon as they go home, they will grow beards. They said they had to shave while they are here because of the police academy rules. Have you ever noticed their hands, Grandma? Their nails are always trimmed and clean, too! I think it's all the Wudu' (washing before the five obligatory daily prayers) they do," Rose said very seriously.

"I was reading in the *What Islam Is All About* book that their Prophet Muhammad taught the Muslims that being clean and dressing nicely pleases God," said Grandma.

"And having good manners, too," chimed in Rose.

"Enough! No more delaying your homework," Grandma said with a stern look in Rose's direction.

Rose scurried to her book bag and got the science worksheet from the homework folder. "Homework! Yuck!" sighed Rose.

The school week seemed to fly by. Rose, Camelia, Ruby, and Christine chattered all week long, through recess and lunch, about the field trip they were taking with their class on Saturday. Rose had finally found her rock-collecting bag. She put the bag, a water bottle, sunscreen, and Grandpa's first-aid kit into a backpack; ready to go for Saturday.

Saturday finally arrived, with the sun shining and only a few fluffy clouds scattered in the blue Arizona sky. "It's going to be a fantastic day for rock hunting," Rose said to her dad as she gobbled her cereal and then emptied her juice glass in one last huge gulp.

"Don't forget to learn something about the Meteorite Crater. I bet you will have to write a paper about your trip or you'll have a quiz about it in class on Monday," cautioned Dad.

"Thanks for reminding me. I'll get my pencil and notepad and put them in my bag," said Rose.

Rose kissed and hugged her dad goodbye when she heard Grandpa honking the horn on his truck as he pulled into the driveway at Rose's house. Grandpa had to pick up Camelia, Christina, and Ruby before going to the school. Students, teachers, and teacher assistants (parents) were riding the school bus to the Meteorite Crater. Rose was sooo excited because she had never ridden on a school bus before. Grandma and Grandpa always drove her to the private Christian school she went to before starting the fifth grade at the public school this year.

"All ready to go?" Grandpa asked as Rose climbed into the front seat of the pick-up truck.

"I'm ready, Spa-ghet-ti!" giggled Rose.

After picking up Rose's friends, Grandpa drove to the school parking lot. Rose and her three friends piled out of the truck with their backpacks and sack lunches. A group of their classmates saw them and hollered, "Hijab-Ez!"

Rose, Camelia, Ruby, and Christina hollered back, "Hijab-Ez!" and waved back.

Moments later, their teacher called everyone to line up to board the school bus. The boys got on first and went to the back of the bus. The parent assistants got on next, followed by all the girls. Everyone's backpacks and lunches were stored at the back of the bus. The travel to Meteorite Crater would take two hours. Rose and her friends brought books, word search puzzles, and crosswords to work to help pass the time.

The Hijab-Ez watched as their teacher, Mrs. Rodriguez, began scolding the boys. The boys were throwing paper wads, and the bus wasn't even out of the parking lot yet!

Camelia shared a seat with Rose, and Ruby and Christina sat behind them. "Did you bring your rock-collecting bag?" asked Camelia.

"Shish! Quiet! I don't want everyone to know I am going rock hounding. This is too good an opportunity to pass up to find some super-de-duper rocks," Rose whispered to her friend.

"But, will you have time to look for rocks? We are supposed to listen to the park ranger and take notes," Camelia whispered back.

"I will listen and take notes, but I am going to find some great rocks, too!" Rose whispered determinedly. Rose's tone of voice and the intense look on her face told Camelia that trouble might be afoot!

Ruby also saw the look on Rose's face and whispered to Christina, "I think Rose is planning something and it just might be trouble with a capital T!"

"How are you going to go rock hounding? The teacher and parent assistants will be watching us all the time so we don't get lost," Christina lowered her voice to a mere whisper.

"Shish! I'm thinking," Rose scolded. Rose reached into her pants pocket and pulled out the brochure about the Meteorite Crater. The teacher had sent one home with each student. The brochure had a map of the park, the Crater, and the Meteorite Museum where they would have lunch in the museum cafeteria. Rose studied the map.

"I've got it!" she exclaimed softly. "I have a PLAN!"

"Rose you always come up with a PLAN. I hope we don't get into any problems," said Christina, with a frown and wrinkled brow signaling how worried she was.

Christina was the worrier in the Hijab-Ez friendship group. She had two older brothers and two younger sisters in her family. She had to help her mother with her younger sisters after school each day. Her mother worked, so Christina had to do many of the household tasks for her mother. Her older brothers didn't help much and, whenever she wanted to go with them, they told her they didn't want a little sister tagging after them. Whenever something happened to her little sisters, her parents always asked Christina what happened because she was the oldest of the girls. Her parents would not be happy if she got into any trouble on this field trip. Christina's parents did not make a lot of money, and everyone in her family had to sacrifice so she could pay the money for this field trip.

Christina was sometimes abrupt with her friends when they did things together. She worried because she didn't have nice clothes like Ruby and Rose. Christina liked hanging out with Camelia, because Camelia always wore baggy, loose clothes. Camelia never seemed to worry very much about what people were wearing or what they looked like. She always said that "pretty is as pretty does!" Camelia explained that Muslims think people are more important than what their clothes look like or how much money they have.

Christina sighed softly and thought, *I'm glad my friends don't mind if the clothes I wear are hand-me-downs or from the Goodwill second-*

hand store. Christina never invited her friends to her home because she lived in an apartment in a poor neighborhood. Sometimes it wasn't safe to play outside. Christina was really looking forward to this trip so she could get out of the city and see the countryside.

"Don't worry, Christina. When everyone sits down to eat lunch, I am going to get excused to go to the restroom. Instead of going to the restroom, I am going to go outside and look for rocks," whispered Rose.

Rose looked at the shocked expressions on her friends' faces and said rather stubbornly, "None of you need to go with me."

"You can't go outside all by yourself!" Camelia exclaimed as worry lines creased her forehead.

The Hijab-Ez were loyal to each other. "We'll go with you," Ruby, Christina, and Camelia whispered almost in unison.

"You and Ruby have to stay and talk to my Grandpa and keep him busy," Rose said to Christina. Rose didn't want Christina to get into any trouble with her parents. "Ruby, you should stay with Christina. Your Mom was real worried about you going on this field trip. If you do anything to get the teacher upset, your mom won't let you go on any more field trips. Camelia can come with me if she wants to." Rose looked questioningly at Camelia sitting across the seat from her.

Ruby and Christina looked relieved and agreed. Camelia said nervously, "You aren't going to climb down into the crater, are you?"

"No, don't be worried about that! I am only going to look around on the ground around the museum. You don't have to go outside with me, just stand at the door and let me know when everyone is finished with lunch," Rose answered confidently.

Camelia didn't like this PLAN. She thought Rose could get hurt and helping her would be disobeying the rules of staying in your group with your group leader. Camelia struggled within herself. She wanted to help Rose, but she didn't want either of them to get into any problems or maybe get hurt! *I can't let Rose go outside alone,* Camelia thought anxiously.

Rose stared stubbornly at Camelia and waited expectantly for Camelia's reply.

"O…kay," whispered Camelia with serious misgivings in the tone of her voice. Rose was so excited about her PLAN that at first she didn't notice her friend's tone of voice or how quiet Camelia had become.

Rose looked quickly at her friend, and then looked away. Suddenly, she began to feel a little uneasy as she looked at the serious expressions on the faces of her friends, but she quickly pushed the feeling back and said, "Friends?"

All four girls raised their pinkie fingers and intertwined them. They whispered, "Hijab-Ez! Friends forever!" and smiled at each other.

Camelia and Ruby took out their books and began reading. Christina sat next to the window and eagerly watched the countryside.

Rose began working on a half-finished Seek 'N Find puzzle, but she couldn't concentrate. Rose had acted brave and confident in front of her friends, but secretly she was a little afraid. She didn't want to think about what would happen if she got caught disobeying the rules. From somewhere locked away in her memories, a key turned, and Rose thought of a story Grandma had told her last year.

Grandma said that when she was a young girl, she had been very poor. All the girls in her class were wearing cute animal pins, and she really wanted to have a pin and be like the other girls. On a Saturday, Grandma went to a local Five and Dime store where the pins were sold. She didn't have any money, so she decided she would take a pin without paying for it.

Rose remembered gasping in astonishment when she heard her grandma talk about stealing!

Grandma said that just as she was about to hide the pin in one of her dress pockets, she heard a big commotion in the front of the store. The owner was arguing with a lady. He was telling her to pay for the things she had stuffed into her purse or he would call the police!

Grandma said she quickly dropped the pin and hurried out of the store. For months, she couldn't go to the store because she felt guilty. Even though she hadn't stolen anything, she might have. She was given a second chance to decide. Grandma told Rose that whenever she thought about doing something wrong, she should remember that once done, she could not go back and undo the wrong. It was better to decide to do the right thing.

Rose shook her head and mumbled to herself, "I won't get caught! My PLAN is perfect!" Deep inside Rose, a small voice whispered, "Don't do it, Rose!" Rose picked up her pencil and looked at the puzzle. She was determined to ignore the whispering voice that was her conscience.

The miles seemed to fly by, and Christina felt a twitch of disappointment when the bus pulled into a huge asphalt parking lot. She loved looking at the open desert and mountains.

"We're here! Once everyone is out of the bus, form up with your group and teacher assistant. I want each of you to stay in your group and not wander off. We will meet at the museum cafeteria at noon. Be sure to write some good notes and have fun," Mrs. Rodriguez instructed her students.

Rose, Camelia, Christina, and Ruby got off the bus and stared. Not one tree! Not one shrub! Everything everywhere appeared to be flat! The sky looked like it was sitting on top of the ground. There was one very large building in the middle of the parking lot. Rose looked beyond the building and counted fifteen signs made like hands with a pointing finger. Each sign was posted at the beginning of a separate path.

Beyond the museum building, Rose saw the flat plain begin to rise. It looked like a hill or even a small mountain. Nothing was growing on it, just rocks and desert sandstone.

"Let's choose a path and get started," said Grandpa. The girls continued to stare with amazement at the landscape. Grandpa found the girls' backpacks, and took his movie camera and binoculars from his own backpack.

"Ready?" Grandpa asked the staring Hijab-Ez. Each girl took her backpack. They huddled together and whispered for a few seconds, and then they all headed for sign number nine.

Grandpa and the girls walked for about twenty minutes, occasionally looking at their classmates walking on the other paths. All the paths headed in the same direction. The farther they walked, the wider the distance between the different numbered paths.

"Look, another sign," said Ruby, pointing to a yellow sign in the distance. As they got closer to the sign, Ruby read out loud what was printed on it: CAUTION! Stay on the path. Do not leave your group.

About one hundred few feet from this sign, the path looked like it came to a dead end. The girls walked to the end of the path, and then stood motionless. Grandpa chuckled when he looked at the Hijab-Ez. Their mouths' were open and they were speechless. Finally, they found their voices.

"Wow!" said Ruby.

"Can you believe it?" Christina said, the wonderment unmistakable in her voice.

"Awesome!" Rose said.

"Subhanallah (Glory be to Him, the Almighty)!" Camelia exclaimed.

In front of the girls was a huge crater. It was so wide (one mile) that they had to use Grandpa's binoculars to see across to the opposite side. The crater was very deep (almost six hundred feet), too. Rose looked at it in astonishment. She saw hundreds of different shaped rocks and huge boulders. The rocks and boulders seemed to be exploding in blotches of desert color: tan, deep brown, light brown, light orange, reddish orange, and black. While looking through the binoculars, Camelia squealed with delight as she spotted a deer and a rabbit. Rose thought she must be very close to the heavens...*a meteorite from space! Space Rocks! Super!*

"Everyone ready for the climb down?" asked Grandpa. He was smiling because of the awestruck look on each girl's face. "When we get halfway down, there will be some benches and we can rest and drink some water. If you get tired before then, let me know." Along the path down to the bottom of the crater were signs that told hikers the facts about the crater. Each of the girls paused to take notes before continuing down the path.

Climbing out of the crater took longer, and the girls had to stop to rest four times. Finally, they made it back to the top of the crater. It was time for lunch, and the girls said they were starving! They hurried to the museum cafeteria and sat with Grandpa and another group of girls and their teacher assistant. Soon, Grandpa was busy in conversation with Mr. Garrett, the other teacher assistant.

"Excuse me. It's time for my Dhuhr prayer," said Camelia as she stood up and walked to the girls' restroom. After making her intention and wudu', Camelia walked to a quiet room off the hallway and said her prayer. Before she finished her prayer, she asked Allah to help her convince Rose not to go outside and hunt for rocks by herself.

When she returned to the lunch table, Camelia heard Ruby ask Rose hopefully, "Did you find any good rocks on the trail to the crater?"

"Yes," said Rose. "There are two beauties right next to the beginning of the path before we walked to the crater edge. I was going to get them when we climbed back up, but Grandpa told me to hurry as we were going to be late for lunch with the group."

Camelia looked at her lunch but was so worried she didn't bother to eat any of it.

"So, you are going ahead with your PLAN?!" Christina whispered with a hint of trepidation in her voice.

"Yes," whispered Rose as she stood, tapped Grandpa on the shoulder to get his attention, and told him she was going to the restroom.

"Coming with me, Camelia?" questioned Rose.

Camelia stood up and reluctantly followed Rose.

"Be careful," mumbled Ruby. She kept her head lowered and for once wasn't interested in the food in front of her.

Christina sat quietly and nervously bit down on one of her fingernails as she watched Rose and Camelia walk away.

Rose and Camelia headed for the restroom. They looked back over their shoulders and saw that Grandpa had his back to them and was now busy talking to Ruby and Christina.

Rose squeezed Camelia's hand. "Now or never," she said with excitement and something else in her voice. They ducked around the corner and headed down the long hallway to the Exit sign above the back door of the museum.

Rose was breathless as she got to the door and pushed it slightly open. She turned and looked back at a solemn-faced Camelia.

"Don't go too far," Camelia squeaked nervously. "Stay close enough so I can see you!" Under her breath she whispered, "*Hafitha-ha, ya Allah*," which means, "May Allah protect and preserve her."

Rose hesitated at the door and looked back at Camelia. Rose's hesitation was all Camelia needed to act. She rushed over to Rose and pleaded, "Rose, please, please, don't go outside!"

Rose stood there a moment with a look of indecision on her face. Suddenly, the indecision disappeared, and Rose said in a firm voice, "This is a bad PLAN. I want those rocks, but I don't want my family to be disappointed with me. I don't want to worry my friends or get them into trouble, either!"

Camelia heaved a big sigh of relief and said, "You could get hurt. I'm glad you decided not to go outside to rock-hound by yourself!"

"So am I," Rose exclaimed and exhaled another sigh of relief. It felt like a big mountain had lifted from her heart. Rose smiled at Camelia and grabbed her hand. They raced back down the hallway and skidded to a stop as they rounded the corner to the lunchroom. Ruby saw them first and hurried to meet them. Grandpa had sent her to see what was taking Rose and Camelia so long in the restroom.

Christina jumped up from the table and walked quickly to where Camelia, Rose, and Ruby were whispering in a huddle.

"Rose didn't go outside after all," said Ruby to Christina.

"It was a bad PLAN," said Rose. The girls hugged each other and walked to their table.

Grandpa whispered to Rose as she sat down next to him. "Here comes a big surprise. I know you are going to like it!"

Mrs. Rodriguez introduced a second park ranger. His name was Ranger John. "I have a surprise for all the rock hounds in your group," he said. "How many of you are rock hounds?"

Rose and six of her classmates raised their hands. "While Ranger Mike takes the rest of the class on a tour of the museum, I am taking the rock-hounders outside to look for some special rocks they can take home today."

Rose and her friends just stared at each other in surprise and disbelief! They had narrowly escaped trouble! Now, Rose would still get to collect rocks!

Grandpa hugged Rose and told her he would be going with her friends to tour the museum. Rose walked over to join the smaller group with Ranger John.

Ruby, Camelia, and Christina walked with Grandpa and the larger group towards the museum. Rose's friends turned, looked back at her, and called out to her.

"Have fun," said Ruby

"Find a beauty," said Christina

"Alhamdulillah (All praise be to Allah)," said Camelia.

"Thank you, Grandma," Rose murmured as she waved to her friends.

❧

The week following the field trip to the Meteorite Crater was a busy one for Rose and the Hijab-Ez. On Monday, their teacher gave them an assignment to write a story about their field trip. (Just like Rose's dad had said she would!) Rose wrote about the great rocks she had brought back with her. One rock had orange and brown markings that look just like lightning bolts. Rose described the composition of the rock (the park ranger told her this information), and she made up a fictionalized story about how the rock came to be at the crater site. The rest of the week, her class was busy because it was "Keep Our School Clean

Week," and the Hijab-Ez had signed up for keeping the art room clean all week.

Christina was cranky all week long. Every day at lunch, she complained about her two young sisters being sooo much trouble. Christina had to babysit her sisters after school each day until her mother got home from work. Thursday, Christina was like a thundercloud ready to burst! The Hijab-Ez were talking about Spring Break the following week and what they would be doing. Rose was going fishing with her dad. Camelia and her family were spending almost the entire week visiting relatives in North Carolina. Ruby was signed up for art classes at the Boys and Girls Club for the whole week. Christina wasn't going any place or doing anything special. All week she had complained about the messes her sisters made and how her parents always blamed her when her little sisters did something wrong. Christina told the Hijab-Ez that her parents said she was responsible for keeping her little sisters out of trouble. Christina said she never had any privacy, had to share her room with her sisters, and even, when they broke her things or messed up the room, her parents always blamed her.

After listening to Christina's complaints all week long, Rose decided that being an only child wasn't such a bad deal, after all. At least she didn't have to share her dad or her grandparents with another person. Getting blamed for the messes and problems younger sisters created was not Rose's idea of happy family relations!

Thursday morning at breakfast, Grandma had some news for Rose. She told Rose her young cousin might be coming to visit them during the spring break. Rose thought, *if Kendall does come to visit, it would be nice for Grandma and Grandpa, because I'm going to be gone on a fishing trip with my dad. What if something happens at Dad's work and he has to cancel our vacation? Oh my gosh!* Rose had another thought. *I wouldn't want to spend the whole week of Spring Break taking care of my cousin Kendall. Not after listening to Christina describe how much trouble five-year-olds can be.*

───── 4 ─────

Big Trouble

Rose, Camelia, Ruby, and Christina finished cleaning the paintbrushes and easels. The Hijab-Ez had volunteered to clean the art room for one week as part of the "Keep Our School Clean Week." The fifth grade classes had split into teams, and each team had picked an area of the school to keep clean during the school's weeklong campaign.

"Now that we finished that icky job, what's next?" Christina wasn't very happy about their decision to clean the art room. She did enough cleaning at home, especially the messes her little sisters made while she was at school!

Rose used her elbow and gently poked Christina's arm. "Stop your grumping. Cleaning the art room is better than picking up trash on the playground for a week!"

"Yuck! I'm glad you didn't sign us up for that job, Rose. Just think of all those sticky candy wrappers with maybe ants crawling on them." Ruby hated to get her hands dirty. She always kept her fingernails filed and polished with light pink enamel. "At least we're cleaning water colors and water-based paste, and not dirt and icky junk," Ruby said in a placating tone of voice.

"The 'Keep Our School Clean Week' was a dumb idea! I wonder what nitwit on the Student Council thought up this idea!" Christina's face looked like a thundercloud as she jabbed a finger at an easel and almost knocked it over.

Camelia had such a hurt look on her face. She was a Student Council member and the campaign was her idea. She bowed her head for a moment to catch her breath and get calm. "It was my idea, and I am sorry you resent helping."

"Wait a minute! Wait a minute!" exclaimed Rose. "I'm the one who signed up the Hijab-Ez. Don't be getting mad at Camelia. You could have erased your name if you didn't want to help!" Rose was getting upset now, too.

Rose, Camelia, and Ruby looked closely at Christina and then at each other. Rose shrugged her shoulders and made a question mark in the air. Camelia pulled on one end of her hijab scarf, something she always did when she was worried or thinking hard about something.

Camelia took a deep breath, walked over to Christina, and gave her a hug. "Why are you in such a bad mood? We've been doing this all week, and today is the last day. Remember TGIF? Thank God It's Friday?"

"Yeah, this is it! Done, kaput, finished!" Rose smiled at her grumpy friend and tried to get Christina to smile back. Ruby was the first to giggle and then it spread to each of the girls with all of them laughing and smiling together.

"Now that we are all back to normal, let's hear it, Christina. What's the problem?" Rose pulled out a chair from one of the tables and sat down. The other girls followed her lead and sat down at the table, too.

"Next week is Spring Break, and I'm stuck at home taking care of my two little sisters. My brothers are going on a camping trip sponsored by our church! What do I get to do? I get to clean up after kids, fix lunches, and dust the house! It's not fair. I wanted to sign up for classes like Ruby did at the Boys and Girls Club, but no way. My dad said they couldn't pay for a babysitter and the classes. Just because they are boys, my parents don't think my brothers should do babysitting. They get to go to camp, and there is money for them! Why can't my brothers babysit for a change? Then I could go to the classes. What about ME?" Christina's voice broke and small tears gathered in her eyes and slowly trickled down her cheeks.

"Didn't you tell us your mom saves money for the family because you babysit your sisters?" Camelia said gently as she put her arm around Christina's shoulders.

"I understand that," sniffed Christina. "But I get tired of watching my little sisters after school every day, and I don't get to join any clubs or visit my friends, either."

"Well, I'd like to have a mom so I could help her," said Rose.

Rose's three friends looked at her and felt sad for Rose, but didn't know what to say to her about the loss of her mother.

Ruby leaned forward with her elbows resting on the table and her chin cupped in her hands. "I know what you mean about never getting to do anything. Every day after school, I have to go to my great aunt's house and wait for my mom to get off work. Aunt Tey is very fussy. She doesn't allow me to play in any of the rooms or make any messes. She likes everything to be in its place. She won't let me play outside, either, because she says she has to watch me so I am safe. Mostly, I just sit and read, but sometimes I want to sing, make paper flowers, or take a walk. During Spring Break, I will have to stay with my Aunt Tey all day long, except for the art class I get to go to each day."

Camelia didn't know what to say. Her family was going to visit relatives during Spring Break, and she knew she would have loads of fun playing with her cousins. She felt sorry for Christina, and Ruby, too. Camelia couldn't think of any way she could help them. She looked at Rose with her big brown eyes signaling "Help!"

Rose hadn't realized how lonely Ruby must get sometimes or how discouraged Christina felt always having to watch her little sisters. Rose didn't have any sisters or brothers and her grandparents lived next door. She always had company or fun things to do with her cat friends. Rose and her dad were going fishing next week. She didn't know how to help her two friends, either.

"I don't know how to help either of you right now. I'll talk to my grandma and call you tonight. We aren't leaving for our fishing trip until Monday."

Christina had calmed down and she looked at Camelia and said, "I'm sorry for saying that stuff about the nitwit and the campaign. I was just upset about Spring Break and all."

"I know you really didn't mean it. Don't worry about it." Camelia smiled at Christina sweetly.

"I'm doomed for a whole week if Rose doesn't come up with a PLAN." Ruby's face now wore its usual calm expression as she looked hopefully at Rose.

Rose raised her right hand, extended her little pinkie finger, and yelled, "Hijab-Ez! Friends forever!"

Her three friends joined her in their friendship call, "Hijab-Ez! Friends forever!"

∾

Rose hurried from the classroom and waved to her friends. She headed for Grandma's car. *I hope Grandma has some ideas to help my friends*, thought Rose. "Hi, Grandma! What's new?"

"I have some happy news. Aunt Tina telephoned and, for sure, your cousin, Kendall, is coming to spend the week of Spring Break with us. You can help me take care of her," replied Grandma as she patted Rose's arm.

Rose's eyes got as big as saucers and a light bulb seemed to pop into her brain flashing off and on. *Warning! Disaster Ahead!* Rose gulped and said, "Grandma, did you forget that Dad and I are going fishing next week?"

"No, I didn't. When your Aunt Tina called and said Kendall would be spending the week with us, I thought you would be excited about having this time with her. I talked to your dad, and he said he would cancel his vacation next week and take you fishing as soon as summer begins."

"I love my cousin Kendall, but I really was looking forward to going fishing with Dad," complained Rose.

"Rose! I'm surprised at you. Your cousin is looking forward to visiting us!"

Grandma's voice sounded disapproving. As Rose peeked up at her face, she saw that Grandma was scowling. Rose didn't say anything. What could she say?!? Rose sat silently remembering what Christina said all the time about how much trouble her little sisters were. Christina described in detail all the messes they made and how she always seemed to get into trouble when her little sisters did something wrong. *Gee Whiz…Kendall is only five years old. What am I supposed to do all day with a five-year-old?* Rose thought. *Dad and I could be fishing, and now I am stuck at home looking after Kendall!*

"But, that's not fair. You didn't even ask me if I wanted to stay home and help take care of Kendall instead of going fishing with my dad," Rose sputtered angrily. *Oops!!* Rose clapped her hand over her mouth. *Too late! Grandma is really frowning now. Oh no! I was gonna ask Grandma to help with Ruby and Christina's problems, and now she's mad at me!*

Grandma looked upset. Her mouth was set in a straight line and her forehead was all scrunched up. Rose knew she had crossed the line.

Grandma didn't answer Rose right away. Rose sat in the back seat and pouted. Grandma calmed down and looked through the rearview mirror at Rose. *Poor Rose, she really looks unhappy.* "Honey, I know you are disappointed. We can have lots of fun with Kendall, and you will still get to go fishing with Dad. Summertime is only a couple of months away."

Rose didn't answer Grandma because she was too mad, and too busy thinking about what Christina had been telling her all week. Then she remembered what Christina had said about her brothers' not having to babysit. "If I was a boy, you wouldn't expect me to help babysit. You wouldn't ask my dad to cancel a fishing trip with his son!" Rose retorted.

Grandma gasped at Rose's angry remarks. "Rose Allen! I'm ashamed of you. Not another word out of you until you apologize." Grandma was thoroughly exasperated with Rose. *I expected Rose to be a little disappointed, but I didn't expect all this anger. Something else must be bothering Rose. I think I better give her some time to cool off,* Grandma thought as she turned the car into the driveway at home.

When Grandma stopped the car, Rose quickly got out and hurried inside Grandma's house. She ran back to her study-playroom and closed the door with a bang!

∾

Rose woke up to a darkened room. She had cried herself to sleep from exhaustion and frustration about her big argument with Grandma. Rose sat up in bed, pushed her tangled hair away from her face, and rubbed the sleep from the corners of her eyes. She glanced at the alarm clock on the bedside table. *Oh no! It's after seven o'clock, and my dad must be home now. Boy, is he gonna be mad at me! What am I gonna tell him? Grandma's probably still mad at me, too!* Like a bolt of lightning flashing across the sky, another thought flashed across Rose's mind. *Kendall will be staying in my room here...Yikes...she'll get into everything!* Rose turned on the night lamp and looked around her room. Her first thought was concern for Jammie, her journal, then her telescope, and then her rock collection. Kendall could mix up the rocks, and then what would Rose do? Another thought struck Rose. *I didn't even think about this when I thought I was going fishing with Dad next week!* Rose got up from her bed, went over to the clothes closet, and opened the doors. The top shelf in the closet was only half full. *Hmmm...I can put my rock collection on the shelf. I think I'll have to ask my dad to carry my telescope over to my house and put it in the sunroom. Jammie can go home with me and stay in my bedroom there.* Rose quickly picked up the first of her ten cookie tins full of her treasures. Using her desk chair as a stepping stool, she placed the cookie tins on the shelf, one by one. When she finished, she looked around the room. Satisfied, she took a deep breath and opened the closed door to her room. *May as well go face the music,* Rose thought with a sick feeling in her stomach. The butterflies were dancing madly in her tummy.

As Rose approached the family room, she could hear the voices of her grandma and dad. Her stomach began to rumble. *Not now!* Rose mumbled to herself. She had missed supper and she was hungry. *How can I be hungry when I don't know what my dad is going to say? I'll probably be grounded for life!*

When Rose stepped into the doorway, Grandma and Dad stopped their conversation and looked over at her. Dad patted the couch and motioned for Rose to come sit beside him.

"Did you have a good nap, Rose?" Grandma asked without a smile.

Rose nodded her head.

"Grandma told me you are very upset about not going fishing next week. I can understand your being disappointed, but I don't understand your attitude about your cousin Kendall." Dad looked at Rose with a scowl on his face.

Rose didn't say anything. *What do I say?* she thought. The silence in the room seemed like a heavy blanket covering Rose, and it made her feel almost as if she was being smothered.

Dad waited a few moments longer, and, when Rose didn't respond, he said in a harsh sounding voice, "If you don't want to talk about this, I can't make you, Rose. You will apologize to your grandmother, do you understand me?"

Rose looked at her dad and then at her grandma. Neither one was smiling. *They don't care what I think. They already made their decisions without even asking me.* Rose said half-heartedly, "I'm sorry for speaking like I did, Grandma."

Grandma and Dad both raised their eyebrows at the unfriendly apology. Grandma was now getting concerned. *Rose never acts like this. Something is really bothering her,* she thought.

Dad sighed in exasperation with Rose. The older Rose got, the harder it seemed for him to understand her.

"I left a plate of sandwiches, a glass of milk, and some cookies on a tray in the refrigerator. Why don't you get your supper and eat? We'll talk about this tomorrow," Grandma suggested.

She nodded towards her son, and he nodded back. *Maybe Rose needed a little more time before she felt ready to talk about this,* Dad thought.

Rose escaped from the family room and got her supper from the refrigerator. She carried the tray back to her study-playroom and set it down on her desk. Rose didn't start to eat right away. Her mind was in a turmoil. *I love my cousin Kendall...Grandma and*

Dad probably think I don't after this big argument. Oh no! I was supposed to call Ruby and Christina this evening. I wonder if they called me. Grandma didn't say anything.

Rose nibbled half-heartedly on her sandwich and tried to think what she could say to her grandma and dad. She needed Grandma's help, too. Rose jumped when she heard the knock on her door. She looked back and saw the door open. Dad was standing in the doorway.

"When you finish supper, I want you to take your shower and spend the night here. I have a lot of reports to do tonight for work tomorrow. We'll talk again when I get home from work. I hope by tomorrow you decide you want to tell me what has caused you to have this attitude about your cousin. Come give me a hug, Rose."

Rose got up from the chair and walked slowly over to her dad. As he hugged her, Rose wished she could talk to him. *I think I need to get things straightened out between me and Grandma first.*

When Dad left, Rose got her nightgown from the battered dresser drawer and went to the bathroom to shower. *While showering, Rose came to a decision. I'll just tell Grandma everything Christina said and see what she says. Maybe Grandma will understand why I'm worried about Kendall coming to stay here.*

After showering, Rose got the tray of barely eaten supper and took it to the kitchen. When she had disposed of the food remains, she went to the family room where Fahd, Abdul, and Grandma were talking about Islam.

Rose hesitated in the doorway and was about to go back to her study-playroom when Grandma spoke, "There you are. Come in and join us, Rose."

"As-Salaam'Alaykum, Little sister," Fahd and Abdul greeted Rose.

"Wa'alaykum as-Salaam," Rose replied and smiled tentatively at Grandma and her Saudi brothers.

Ring! Ring!

"I'll go answer the telephone," Grandma said. She got up from the recliner. As she walked by Rose, she patted her gently on the shoulder.

Rose sat down in the recliner Grandma had vacated and looked at Fahd and Abdul. *Maybe I should talk to them about this big problem?*

Before Rose could say anything, Abdul said, "Little Sister did not have a very good day?"

Rose nodded her head in agreement.

"Your grandma said you are unhappy about not going fishing next week with your dad and you are upset about helping care for your little cousin, is this so?"

Rose nodded her head again.

"Fahd thinks this is not why you are very upset. He thinks you like your little cousin. Fahd thinks you did not tell your grandma why you got angry," Abdul said, and Rose saw Fahd nod his head and smile gently at her.

Abdul patted the couch where he and Fahd were sitting, and Rose quickly went to the couch and sat down between them. "You will tell your big brothers what is making Rose feel bad and say sad things to Grandma and Dad, right?" Fahd said gently.

Tears glistened in Rose's eyes as she told Fahd and Abdul what Christina had said about her little sisters and described all the problems Christina got into because of the things her little sisters did. Rose explained that she felt hurt when her grandma and dad hadn't asked if she minded not going on the fishing trip first, before they made their decision. Rose said, "I don't understand why boys get treated better than girls. If I was a boy, my grandma probably never would ask my dad to cancel our fishing trip. Maybe girls aren't as important as boys? I don't know what to say to Dad or Grandma. My friends were counting on me to ask Grandma to help them during Spring Break. Now, I can't ask Grandma because she is really mad at me. Dad, too."

Rose was not aware that Grandma had finished her telephone call and was standing just outside the family room doorway listening to Rose's conversation with Fahd and Abdul. As Grandma listened to Rose, she remembered all the small trips and activities Rose's dad had planned for them and had to cancel because of work. She remembered his promise to take her fishing once before and how her son had gone fishing with his buddies instead. Grandma realized that she had handled everything very poorly. Rose was right about one thing. She should have talked things over with Rose before asking her son to cancel the fishing trip next week. She should have given Rose the opportunity to make a choice between visiting with her cousin or going fishing with her dad. Grandma remained silent and waited to see what her Saudi boys would say to Rose.

Abdul was the first to speak. "Rose must make a good apology to her dad and grandma. I think you did not make a good one already?"

Rose smiled sheepishly and nodded.

"Good! This is decided. You must always speak good words to your parents, even when you do not agree, right?"

Again Rose nodded her head in agreement.

"I would tell Grandma and Dad you got mad because they did not tell you about their idea of you helping with your little cousin. It is okay to feel disappointment about the fishing trip, Little Sister. It is not okay to speak in angry words. When you are angry, you say other words you do not mean, is this not so?" Abdul asked.

"Yes. I was so busy thinking about what Christina had said, I got upset and didn't tell Grandma why I was worried."

"So...Rose will tell Grandma and Dad about your friend Christina and what you worry about?"

Rose looked stricken.

"What is troubling you, Rose?"

"I think they won't listen to my side. They won't understand," Rose said and sighed.

"Rose has much trust with Dad and grandparents. Right? So, you will trust them and talk to them," Abdul concluded. He smiled encouragingly at Rose.

Once again, Rose nodded agreement.

Fahd had been silent all this time and he cleared his throat and spoke next. "I think Little Sister has made a mistake about her grandma and dad."

Rose looked at Fahd with surprise. Fahd had never said anything like this to her before.

"I see last summer Grandma and Rose's dad being very kind to her cousins, EJ, Mike, and Chris, when they visit and they go on the trip to the Grand Canyon with us. Rose's grandma and dad treat Rose with the same kindness, is this not so?"

Rose nodded her head in agreement.

"Islam teaches that girls and boys are to be treated with the same kindness and fairness. Boys are not better because they are stronger or because they are boys. There are many famous Muslimahs that all Muslims admire much and have great respect for. There are many women in your country's history that were brave and smart, same as many men. Rose must not think this wrong idea about Grandma and Dad. It is not so," Fahd said firmly, but smiled gently at Rose.

"I'll tell my dad and grandma I'm sorry for saying that stuff about boys. You are right, Fahd."

"This is a good idea, Little Sister. I think Fahd may have a story to tell Little Sister. Maybe it will be a story about a famous Muslimah?" Abdul said as he smiled at Rose and nodded to Fahd.

"Story? Did I hear someone say Fahd is going to tell us a story?" Grandma entered the family room smiling and pretended as though she had just finished her telephone call.

Rose looked at Grandma and they exchanged smiles. *First thing tomorrow I'm gonna talk to Grandma and then to my dad when he gets home from work,* Rose promised herself.

"I will tell Rose one very small story. It is getting late, and Abdul and I must go to class tomorrow to practice with handcuffs." Fahd said this and made a silly face. Fahd and Abdul didn't have much experience with the newest arrest procedures they were being taught at the police academy. Grandpa was helping them with this each morning after the boys said Fajr prayer. Grandpa didn't mind the early morning hours as he was always up before the birds anyways.

"This story is about a very famous Muslimah who lived in my country many years ago. My country and all Muslims everywhere honor her for being kind, generous, and courageous. She loved Allah and was a loyal and caring member of her family. This

Muslimah fought in battles against idol worshipers. She was very brave. I call her the 'Woman Warrior'."

Rose clapped her hands in anticipation.

"Many hundreds of years ago, the Muslims were living in peace. They had some neighbors who worshiped idols. These neighbors decided they did not like the Muslims and wanted to take the homes and land of the Muslims. Prophet Muhammad (pbuh) was the leader of the Muslims and he told his people they would have to fight the idol worshipers.

"One fight was the Battle of *Uhud*. While the men were fighting, the Muslim women helped by bringing them water and cleaning the wounds of the Muslim men who got hurt. During the fighting, the men began to climb a hill and didn't pay attention to the Prophet (pbuh) who was behind them. He called them to come back as they were needed to fight some idol worshippers attacking and surrounding the Prophet (pbuh) and the group with him.

"*Nasibah*, the mother of *Umarah*, saw some men trying to kill the Prophet (pbuh). She grabbed a sword and used it and a bow with arrows to defend him against their enemies. She received a deep wound on her shoulder from an enemy's sword that day. While fighting, she saw the man who wounded her son and she killed him. That day, she received many wounds but she did not die. The Prophet (pbuh) told her that she would be in Paradise because of her courage and for saving his life. This news made her very happy.

"Nasibah went on to fight during other battles and she was present when treaties were made, too. When the Prophet (pbuh) died, Nasibah remained a warrior and fought many battles under the new leader, Abu Bakr. At the Battle of *Al-Yamamah*, she was wounded eleven times and lost one of her hands!"

Rose gasped when she heard this. Abdul and Fahd grinned at each other.

"She was held in high esteem by all Muslim leaders of her time. Nasibah was also one of the first seventy-three people who became Muslim and she gave her allegiance to the Prophet (pbuh) before the Muslims moved from Makkah to Madinah.

Madinah became the home city of the Prophet, and he is buried in this city. So, Little Sister, you can see that women can be brave and strong and do many things that men do. Women are as good as men. Today, Muslimahs do not go to battle because there is not a need for this in Muslim countries. There are more Muslim men in our present time, and Allah has said men must be the protectors of women."

Fahd ended his story and grinned. He loved telling stories about famous Islamic people and the history of Islam.

"Please, Fahd. Just one more story," Rose pleaded. Already she felt better and her big problem didn't seem quite so big any more.

"One more story, and then Fahd and Abdul must get some sleep and you too, young lady," Grandma said gently and smiled at Rose.

Fahd didn't complain about telling another story. He rubbed his hands together in anticipation. Storytelling was one of the things he and his family loved to do every night at his home in Saudi.

"My second story is about the daughter of the Prophet (pbuh). Her name is *Fatimah*. She loved her father very much, and people often said she had the good manners and same way of speaking as the Prophet (pbuh). Fatimah was respected because she was a patient, generous, and kind daughter.

"She married Ali after the Battle of *Badr*. This was a big battle between the new Muslims and the idol worshippers who didn't like the new Muslims. Many Arab people worshipped idols and were mad at Prophet Muhammad (pbuh) because he told them this was wrong. He told them they should only worship the one true God, Allah, who made the world and everything in it.

"One day, some very mean idol worshipers saw Prophet Muhammad (pbuh) saying his prayer. They took some bloody camel guts and threw them on his back as he was on his hands and knees bowing to God. These mean people stood laughing at the Prophet (pbuh). Fatimah saw what they did to her father. She ran to him and quickly cleaned off the horrible camel guts and defended her father against the mean idol worshipers.

"Years later, when her father was very ill, Fatimah didn't leave his side. She took care of him every day. She was very sad because her father grew weaker and weaker. Her father tried to comfort her by whispering something to her. It was a secret. When Fatimah heard the secret she cried at first. Then the Prophet (pbuh) whispered again to her and Fatimah laughed."

Rose raised her hand and Fahd said, "Yes, Rose, what do you want to ask?" Fahd smiled at Rose. He had been expecting her to ask a question. Rose always asked him questions in the middle of his stories!

"What is the secret he told her?"

"He told her that the Angel Gabriel made him recite the Qur'an twice that year. This meant that he would die and not be alive the next year. Fatimah began to cry when she heard her father's words. Then the Prophet (pbuh) whispered again in her ear and she smiled. He told her that she would be the leader of women believers in Paradise!

"Everyone wanted to know what the Prophet (pbuh) had told his daughter, but she would not tell anyone until after her father died. Six months after her father died, Fatimah got sick and died. She went to heaven to be with her father." Fahd smiled again as he finished his story.

"Do you understand, Little Sister, that girls and boys are the same to Allah? Also to your dad and your grandma?" Abdul asked again.

Rose nodded and sneaked a look at Grandma. Grandma was looking at her and smiling. Grandma nodded her head to Rose.

"Time for bed everyone."

Fahd, Abdul, and Rose got up from the couch and each one said their goodnights to Grandma. Rose hurried back to her study-playroom. She was sleepy and wanted to say her prayers before going to sleep.

❧

Rose tried to move her right foot but couldn't. *Something is pulling my foot*, Rose thought sleepily as she tried to stretch, but her foot still wouldn't move. Rose opened her sleepy eyes and saw Dad standing at the foot of her bed, grinning at her and holding her foot. "Time to get up, knucklehead!"

"Daddy!" Rose squealed. "What are you doing here?"

"I decided to take today and tomorrow off from work. My boss said it was okay since I won't be going on vacation next week. Hurry up and get dressed in some old jeans and a shirt. You and I are going fishing today at the Tempe Town Lake."

Rose couldn't believe her ears. Last night, Dad and Grandma were really upset with her. Today, she had been planning to explain everything to Dad when he got home; apologize, too! Before Rose could say anything more, Dad said, "Your grandparents and I will be waiting for you in the dining room. Hurry up, now. Time is a-wasting and the fish are biting!"

Rose was met by three smiling faces when she got to the dining room. Grandpa patted the chair next to him and said, "Good morning, Rose, how about some eggs and toast?"

"Good morning, Grandma and Grandpa. I'm hungry, and eggs sound good!" Rose replied.

"I'm going next door to get our fishing gear ready. Grandma wants to talk to you a few minutes, Rose. When she's through, meet me back at our house." Dad ruffled Rose's tangled hair and gave his mom a peck on the cheek before heading out the front door.

While Rose ate her eggs, Grandma apologized to her for not giving her a choice about the fishing trip. Rose was so surprised she almost choked on her toast. Grandma's kind words and apology were all Rose needed to spill out all her worries about babysitting Kendall, and her worries that boys are better than girls.

Grandma and Grandpa didn't interrupt her while she poured out all the stuff that had been bothering her. Rose finished by explaining about her promise to try and help Ruby and Christina. She told Grandma how lonely Ruby would be over Spring Break, and how unhappy Christina was because she had to babysit her little sisters the whole week. "Grandma, will Kendall make lots of messes? I don't know what I can do with a five-year-old kid, either. Can we do anything to help my friends?" Rose asked in a rush of words. She looked hopefully at Grandma.

Grandma hugged Rose. "I can see now why you were upset, Rose. I have a simple solution to the problems your friends have next week. We can invite them to spend each day with us. Christina can bring her little sisters. I am sure Kendall will like meeting them. I will call their parents and make the arrangements. Don't be worried about your cousin Kendall. I am taking next week off from work, so I will be at home to help with her and help Christina with her sisters."

"Thanks, Grandma. I was worried about asking you because I was so rude yesterday. I thought you wouldn't help me. Silly me," giggled Rose.

"You are a silly goose," agreed a smiling Grandma. "I 'accidentally' overheard you talking to Abdul and Fahd last night when I came back from my telephone call. This morning, I called your dad, and we both agreed that there was a good solution. This is why your dad is taking today and tomorrow off from work. You and your dad can spend today fishing. Next week, you and I will look after your little cousin."

Rose hugged her grandma and felt like a big weight had been lifted from her heart. "I am really sorry about how mean I acted and talked to you, Grandma. I was going to tell you this first thing this morning. I would have apologized even if you didn't apologize to me and Dad didn't take me fishing."

"I believe you, Sweetie. Let's try and remember for the future. If you are worried or upset, you need to tell Dad, Grandpa, or I what is bothering you. Remember, you have only heard Christina's side of her problem, too. Maybe this week we can get Christina to talk with us again and we can find some ways to help her get along better with her little sisters. Want to try?"

Rose nodded her head and finished her glass of juice. "Do you want to go fishing with Dad and me, Grandpa?" Rose asked politely.

Grandpa had been silent during the conversation, ready to help if needed. He was happy to see things were better between his wife and Rose, and between Rose and her dad. "I think I'll pass on the invitation. Grandma has some chores for me to do today, and we are going grocery shopping before your Aunt Tina and Cousin Kendall get here tomorrow. Thanks for the invite, Rosie Posie!"

"I'm leaving and I'm going to catch the biggest fish in the lake for our supper!" Rose declared as she headed out the front door.

Around 7:00 PM, Rose and her dad returned home with a stringer full of fish. Rose may not have caught the biggest fish in the lake, but she caught two bass and one large trout. Dad caught three trout, too. Dad cleaned the fish, and Grandpa cooked the fish on the grill outside.

Grandma made a potato salad and coleslaw. Fahd and Abdul were working and weren't home for supper. This was the only thing that kept an almost perfect day from being perfect. Rose ate fish until she felt almost like a stuffed fish!

While they were fishing, Dad talked to Rose about how important she was to him. He also told her that he was very happy God had sent him a little girl because girls were just as special as little boys.

❧

Early Sunday morning, Aunt Tina and Kendall arrived at Grandma's house. Aunt Tina told Grandma she couldn't stay long because of the long drive back home (five hours). Aunt Tina thanked Grandma and Rose for agreeing to care for Kendall.

"I couldn't get any time off from work to take care of Kendall next week. Kendall will be staying with you, and I won't need to leave her with strangers and pay for babysitting. Kendall is very important to me, and I want to thank you, Rose, for helping. I was very worried about having to leave Kendall with strangers."

When Rose heard this, she was glad she was going to do an important job helping her Aunt Tina.

Kendall was carrying Rupert, her favorite stuffed teddy bear. She walked over to Rose and said, "I can spell my last name. It's spelled H-A-R-T, not H-E-A-R-T!"

"You spell real well, Kendall. I like your bear. He's a nice bear. Do you want to come outside with me and meet my cat friends?" Rose asked. Kendall gave Rose an eager smile and nodded her head.

Kendall and Rose went out to the back patio, and Rose introduced her three cat friends. Soon, they were busy swinging on the swing set and talking about going to the park for a picnic the next day. As Rose pushed her little cousin on the swing, her thoughts raced ahead to the next week and Christina. *Maybe I will talk to Christina tomorrow about how important she is to her mother and little sisters. Maybe I'll suggest she talk to her mom about all this stuff with her sisters and brothers that upset her. I wonder if Grandma and I can help Christina. Maybe we can find a way to help Ruby, too. It's going be a long week without seeing my best friend Camelia!*

❧

Spring Break was a smashing success! Rose, Ruby, and Christina were big sisters to Kendall and Christina's little sisters all week long. They played games, did arts and crafts, went to the park twice, and baked cookies. Fahd and Abdul visited with them Thursday afternoon, and Fahd told a story about his first time camping in the desert to the delight of all six girls. Friday, when Rose's friends got ready to go home, something very special happened. After Rose and Grandma took her friends home, Rose hurried to her study-playroom to "chat" with Jammie, her journal, about the special conversation!

5

Names

The next day, Rose sat in the glider with her cat friends. Rose was remembering her special conversation with Christina and Ruby as they got ready to go home yesterday...

Christina, Ruby, and Rose were sitting at the dining room table, waiting while Grandma took the three younger girls to the restroom to wash their hands and faces.

Christina looked at Ruby and then she turned to Rose and said, "I have something important to tell you, Rose. This week, I learned a lot about being kind to my sisters and how much my mom needs my help. I learned lots of new games and crafts I can do with my sisters at home. I have been complaining all year about having to babysit them. I was wrong to resent helping my mother. After this week, I am going to keep doing some of the things we did this week with my sisters. I don't need to be mad about watching them, because I know how to have fun with them. I think they had fun with me, too. They hugged me and kissed me and weren't crying or fighting all the time!"

Ruby spoke up. "I had lots of fun, too. Christina and I talked and decided that if our mothers say it is okay, I am going to go home from school with Christina sometimes to visit and help her play with her little sisters. My Aunt Tey will be happy to have some free days from taking care of me! She will enjoy the peace and quiet when I am at Christina's house!"

It had been a great week because the problems her two friends had were resolved. Christina learned to have fun taking care of her sisters, and Ruby found a way to stop being lonely and bored each day after school. More importantly, Rose had learned to trust her Dad and Grandma, even when she was worried that they might not like or agree with what she might say.

Today, Rose and her family were going to pick the oranges and grapefruits from the trees in Grandma's backyard. Rose had her gloves on and was ready to get to work. The grown-ups were finishing their coffee in the dining room, and Rose waited impatiently to get started on the work! Dad was going to pay her fifty cents for each box she filled with fruit the grownups picked.

Rose wiped her sweaty brow with the sleeve of her shirt. The sun shone brightly on the top of her head, making her hair look like spun gold. Another hour, and everyone would take a break for lunch. Grandpa, Grandma, Fahd, Abdul, Rose, and Rose's dad had spent most of the morning picking the ripe oranges and grapefruit. Rose was assigned the job of bringing water for the thirsty fruit pickers and filling empty boxes with the fruit already picked. Already the back lawn was covered with sweet smelling oranges and large yellow grapefruits.

"Help! I need some help!" exclaimed Rose as she paused to look at the sea of orange and yellow fruit.

Fahd climbed down from one of the ladders propped against the grapefruit tree and smiled at Rose's exasperation. Four fruit pickers and only one fruit boxer just wasn't quite fair!

"I am tired of climbing up and down the ladder. I will help you, Little Rose, with your task," Fahd offered.

Rose looked at Fahd and then burst out laughing. Fahd's hair was full of leaves, and twigs were poking out from the thick curly strands on top of his head.

"I think you look like a tall, skinny tree," giggled Rose as she pointed at Fahd's head.

"I think I need to take a short rest. Do you want to get us some water?" Fahd asked and then laughed as he began to pick out the twigs and green leaves stuck haphazardly in his curly hair.

Rose went indoors, got two bottles of cold water from the refrigerator, and returned to the patio. The telephone rang just as Rose sat down on the glider. "I'll get it," she called to Grandma as she picked up the telephone receiver. "This is Rose Allen speaking. Just a minute and I'll get my dad. Dad, it's somebody from your work wanting to talk to you," Rose called out.

Rose's dad climbed down the ladder from the grapefruit tree and hurried over to the telephone placed on a table next to the backdoor. Rose sat on the glider, watched her dad, and frowned. *I bet he has to go in to work right now. Every time we are doing something together as a family, his dumb ol' work calls him to go in and fix some problem,* Rose thought dejectedly.

Dad put down the telephone receiver and looked at Rose's unhappy face. He felt awful about what he had to say. "I have to go in to work. An officer has been injured, and I need to conduct the investigation right away. I'm sorry, Rose."

Rose jumped up from the glider and hugged her dad's waist. He was so tall she had to crane her neck as she looked up at him. "Are you coming back today?"

"I'll call if I have to stay over night," Rose's dad called out to Grandma as he opened the back door to leave.

"Be careful, son," Grandma called back.

"Let us know when everything is under control there," Grandpa called out from his perch on a limb in the orange tree.

A few minutes later, Grandma, Grandpa, and Abdul joined Rose and Fahd on the patio.

"Boy, is it getting hot!" exclaimed Grandpa.

"I think it's time to make some lunch. Afterwards, we can box up the rest of the fruit and take it to the food bank in Phoenix," Grandma said as she took off her gloves and opened the back door.

Fahd and Abdul excused themselves, as it was getting close to prayer time, and they needed to get cleaned up before prayer.

Rose went inside with Grandma to help fix lunch while Grandpa busied himself putting away the ladders they had used that morning.

"What does your name mean in Arabic?" Rose asked Grandma as they set the table for lunch.

"I don't know, Rose. I don't think there is an Arabic name for Linda," Grandma replied as she placed a large plate of sandwiches in the middle of the table.

"When Fahd and Abdul finish their prayer, I'm going to ask them." Rose went to the back door and called Grandpa to come in and get ready for lunch.

❧

After everyone finished eating, Grandpa, Abdul, and Fahd finished boxing the fruit they had picked and loaded fifteen boxes into Grandpa's truck. Abdul and Fahd loaded the trunk and back seat of Abdul's car with eight boxes of fruit. Grandpa and Abdul went to deliver the fruit in the truck to a local food bank, while Fahd, Rose, and Grandma drove to the masjid to deliver the boxes of fruit for the Muslim community.

On the drive home, Rose had her first opportunity to ask Fahd about Grandma's name. "Fahd, is there an Arabic name for my grandma's name, Linda?"

Fahd was driving and he looked into the rearview mirror at Rose who was sitting with Grandma in the back seat of the car. "No, Little Rose, there isn't an Arabic word for the name Linda."

"If Grandma lived in Saudi, I mean, was born in Saudi, what name do you think she would have?" Rose asked. She could barely contain her curiosity. It shone through her gray-blue eyes.

Grandma smiled at Rose and said, "I don't think Fahd can answer that question."

"Well, maybe Fahd can tell me what name he would give you, because he knows you and Arabic names, Grandma."

Fahd looked thoughtfully at Grandma for a moment and then said, "I probably would call her *Zaynab*, because of all the crafts your Grandma makes and then gives the money to charity."

"Who is Zaynab?" Rose asked excitedly. *Oh boy, now I'm going to hear another story for sure!*

Fahd turned the corner to the street where Rose lived and said, "I will tell you the story of Zaynab as soon as we get home."

While Grandma, Fahd, and Rose were getting out of the car, Grandpa and Abdul pulled into the driveway. Grandma suggested they go to the back patio, have some raspberry tea, and relax for a while. Everyone was tired after a very busy morning picking fruit.

Rose grabbed Abdul's hand as they walked into the house. "Guess what? Fahd is going to tell us the story about Zaynab because she made crafts and sold them to make money for charity, just like my Grandma does!" exclaimed Rose.

"Yes, your grandma is very generous, like Zaynab," agreed Abdul.

"Fahd says Grandma's name does not have an Arabic word. What name in Arabic do you think would best describe my grandma?" Rose asked Abdul.

"Hmm…I think Zaynab is a nice name, but not the one that best describes your grandma. Perhaps the name *Widad* would be a good nickname. Widad means friendship and love, and your grandma has this in abundance." Abdul looked back at Fahd with an inquiring look on his face.

"Yes! Yes! Widad is a very good name to describe Mum." Fahd nodded his head in agreement with Abdul.

"I think I like the nickname Widad," Grandma said and smiled at her boys.

"It can be your Arabic nickname, Grandma," Rose added.

Everyone got comfortable with their raspberry iced tea and the chocolate brownies Rose and Grandma had made the day before. After Fahd finished one huge chocolate brownie and licked the fingers of his right hand, he took a swallow of his tea and cleared his voice. "Now, I will tell the story of Zaynab.

"Zaynab is a very special person for several reasons, and I will explain them. Zaynab bint Jahsh–this is her full name–and her brother received a proposal of marriage from the Prophet (pbuh) for the Prophet's (pbuh) adopted son, Zayd. Zaynab and her brother didn't want to accept the proposal, but finally agreed because the Prophet (pbuh) asked them to agree. After a while, it was clear to everyone that Zaynab and Zayd did not get along well, and they were unhappy in their marriage. The Prophet (pbuh) felt bad because he remembered that Zaynab and her brother really didn't want this marriage. Zayd then decided to divorce Zaynab. When this happened, the Prophet (pbuh) thought he should propose marriage to Zaynab. He didn't want her to be so sad about what had happened. After the waiting period that must pass after a divorce, the Prophet (pbuh) sent a marriage proposal to Zaynab and her brother. Zaynab did not accept the proposal right away. She sent a message to the Prophet (pbuh) that said she must pray and ask Allah what she should do. This kind of special du'a is called *istikhara*. She told the Prophet (pbuh) that if Allah made the way easy for her to marry him, then she would know it was what Allah wanted her to do."

"What is the waiting period?" Grandma asked when Fahd paused in his story.

"It is called *'iddah*. Islam requires a divorced woman to wait three months after her divorce before she can remarry," Abdul answered for Fahd.

Fahd thanked Abdul and then continued with his story. "In the meantime, Allah revealed a special verse of the Qur'an, which said that Allah made the marriage contract (Nikkah) between the Prophet (pbuh) and Zaynab. The Prophet (pbuh) went to Zaynab and recited the verse, and, when she heard this, she agreed to marry him. The Prophet had a very large wedding party after his marriage to Zaynab. A wedding party is called a walimah."

"Something else happened, which is very important to Muslims. The verses in the Qur'an about hijab were revealed at this time," Abdul volunteered, and this time Fahd gave him a scowl for the interruption to his story.

"After her marriage, Zaynab would often remind the other wives of the Prophet (pbuh) that Allah made her Nikkah while their Nikkah was made by their parents!

"*A'isha*, one of the Prophet's (pbuh) wives, would tell people that she didn't know any woman better than Zaynab. She was perfect in her belief and loved Allah. Zaynab was very honest in her speech, kind and cordial to her relatives, charitable, and she used to work very hard with her handicrafts so she could give more in charity.

"One day, the Prophet's (pbuh) wives asked him who would be the first wife to join him in Paradise after he died. The Prophet told them it would be the one with the longest hands. This caused all the wives to measure each other's hands to see which one of them had the longest hands. They did not think about the Arabic meaning of longest hands. In Arabic, this expression means generosity. When Zaynab died, she was the first wife to die after the Prophet's (pbuh) death. The other wives realized, as do all Muslims, that Zaynab's generosity was appreciated by Allah and the Prophet (pbuh). The example of Zaynab shows all Muslim women that it is okay to work with ones hands for the good of others. Making crafts for a living or to help others is a very good thing to do." Fahd finished his story and smiled at Rose.

Rose was all smiles as she clapped her hands. "I think that Zaynab is a good name just like Widad is a good name. Which of the names do you like best, Grandma?" Rose asked.

"I'm going to stick with the nickname Widad. I don't feel I could live up to the name of the wonderful Muslimah, Zaynab," Grandma replied and gave Rose a quick hug.

Grandpa had been listening to the story and the conversation about names and hadn't said much of anything. The conversation about names reminded him of his parents. "I have a story I'd like to tell," Grandpa said. Everyone stopped talking and looked at him in surprise.

Wow! Grandpa wants to tell a story! Rose thought as her eyes sparkled with anticipation.

"My grandparents emigrated from Mexico to the United States when they were young and just married. They rode the freight trains all the way to Detroit, Michigan. Eventually, my grandfather got a job in one of the car manufacturing companies.

My dad was born in Michigan, and all the Mexican people lived in a small neighborhood. Everyone spoke Spanish, and my dad never learned to speak English. He only went to the second grade in school.

"When he married my mother, they decided they did not want to live in the busy city, so they made their way to Arizona, picking fruit and doing odd jobs. Both of my parents were very proud to be citizens of the United States, but sad because they could not speak English. My dad worked sixteen to eighteen hours a day in the copper mines of Morenci. He eventually saved enough and bought a small home. My mom was kept busy taking care of the house, me, my brother, and my two sisters.

"When I started kindergarten, I could not speak English. The teachers talked to my parents in Spanish and told them I would not be able to go to first grade until I could speak English and could say and write my A-B-C's. My parents had great respect for teachers, and they wanted me to learn English so I would do well in my life in this country they loved. The first thing I learned to spell and write was my name. It was the Mexican custom for children to be given their mother's last name as a middle name. This is why my middle name is Nunez, my mother's family's last name.

"My teacher told my mother that my middle name was unusual, and that it was not an American custom to give children last names for middle names. That night, my mother sat down at the dining room table to watch me practice writing my name. She made me promise to give my children good American middle names. She told me we were not living in Mexico, and the United States was our country."

"What happened, Grandpa? Did you give Auntie Tina an American name?" Rose asked. Rose never seemed to be able to wait until a story ended before asking questions.

Grandma gave her a quelling look, and Rose squeaked out a "Sorry" to her grandpa.

Grandpa winked at Rose and continued his story. "Many years later, on the night your Auntie Tina was born, my mother made my dad drive her to the hospital where she waited until she saw the nurse write Auntie Tina's name, Tina Michelle, on the nameplate for the nursery crib. She said, "Bien!" which means good, and then told my dad to drive her home." Grandpa smiled as he finished relating a long-ago, fond memory.

Rose got up and hugged her grandpa and said, "I like your story!"

Grandma smiled at her husband and granddaughter and said, "For many years, choosing a new child's name was a very important matter for parents and the entire family. Even today, your name is something that stays with you from the time you are born until you die. Many women change their last name to their husband's last name when they marry, while others decide to keep their birth name. My mother told me that she decided to name me Linda because her favorite movie star at the time I was born was named Linda Darnell!"

"No kidding, Grandma?" Rose exclaimed.

Grandma nodded her head and smiled.

"When a Muslim woman gets married, she does not change her name to her husband's last name. Our Prophet (pbuh) taught that women should keep their own names so they are recognized as individuals. Also, it helps ensure that blood relatives do not marry one another if they should be living in different countries and not know each other very well," Abdul said.

"Muslims usually pick a name based on the meaning of the name. Parents often pick the name of an Islamic historical person they admire greatly," Fahd added.

Abdul said, "We are also fond of choosing nicknames for people. When Muslim women have their first child, they often begin to call themselves by the first name of their first child. My mother's first son is named *Hamza*, so she calls herself *Umm Hamza*, meaning 'mother of Hamza'."

Rose had been listening with great interest and she waited for the chance to ask her question. "Who chose my name, Grandma?"

"Your mother named you Rose after her mother, and your dad named you Lin after me. My friends at work call me by this nickname," Grandma replied and smiled as Rose beamed.

"Did you know my other grandma?" Rose asked hopefully.

"No, I never met her, but she has a lovely name and so do you!"

"My friends and I don't call each other by any nicknames. Do you think we should choose a nickname for each other?" Rose asked the adults listening to her.

"Nicknames are nice, but are not necessary, dear. We sometimes call you different names, such as sweetie pie and honey. These are words to tell you we care about you," Grandma replied.

"My dad calls me a knucklehead sometimes. This is a silly name, or fun name, right?"

"Yes, Rose, and I think your grandpa sometimes calls you Rosie Posie, too!"

Abdul added, "Nicknames are usually given to a person to describe some behavior. Your grandma is kind and loving. Widad is a good nickname for her. You are not our blood sister, but we think of you the same as a sister. This is why Fahd and I nicknamed you Little Sister."

Rose nodded her head in understanding.

"Abdul and I must get ready for evening prayer, Mum. After prayer, we will be coming straight home. I think we will sleep well tonight from all this work!" Fahd said as he and Abdul stood up to leave.

"It's time we all get cleaned up, and Rose needs to practice her piano for her lesson next week," Grandma replied.

～

Rose opened Grandpa's truck door, got out, and closed it quickly. She was excited and had just got home from school. The big excitement was a new school project and she was going to need some help. Rose hurried through the front living room, calling out, "Anybody home?" She went into the family room and then looked through the double French doors to the back patio. Fahd, Abdul, and Grandma were sitting in patio chairs, talking. Rose walked through the kitchen and out the back door.

"As-Salaam'Alaykum," Rose said to Fahd and Abdul, and "Hello," to Grandma.

"Wa'alaykum as-Salaam," replied Fahd and Abdul.

"What are you doing out here?" Rose said in her usual inquisitive tone of voice.

"We are having raspberry iced tea and baklava, and discussing firearms," said Grandma. "Fahd and Abdul need to learn how to take care of their police duty weapon. They will be using a different kind of gun from the weapon they carry on duty in Saudi Arabia. They have to learn how to use a semi-automatic pistol like the one I carry when I am on duty."

"So that's why you have your police gun on the table. But why is your gun in pieces?" Rose asked. Rose seemed to never run out of questions.

"Your grandma was showing us how to clean the gun, take it apart, and then put it back together," said Abdul. "In our country, we do not practice taking our gun apart because it does not come in many pieces."

"There are only a few pieces!" chided Grandma with a warm smile for Abdul.

"We use a revolver for our duty weapon. My revolver only has six bullets, while your grandma's pistol has nine bullets. Most of the bullets are in the clip that must be loaded before putting it into the pistol. We will be learning how to shoot with a semi-automatic pistol like the one your grandma uses for her job," said Abdul.

"We have already finished the lesson from your grandma," added Fahd.

"Well, I didn't teach a good lesson today. Here we are sitting outside having iced tea, while my duty weapon was left lying on the dining room table. I should have put it away, immediately. I am sorry, Rose, for being so careless." Grandma shook her head in dismay at her neglect, got up, and went to the back door. "Always keep your weapons securely locked up when you are not using or cleaning them. I'm going inside to take care of my weapon, pronto!" Grandma exclaimed as she went inside the house.

"Where is your grandpa?" Fahd asked.

"He's getting ready for work," replied Rose.

"Come and sit down with us and have some tea, Little Sister," Fahd said as he patted the other end of Grandma's swing glider.

Rose loved it when Abdul and Fahd called her 'Little Sister.' She didn't have any sisters or brothers and thought of Fahd and Abdul as her big brothers.

"How was your day at school?" asked Grandma as she returned to the patio after safely securing her police weapon.

"Fine! Ruby's parakeet died, but her dad bought her two new ones. She named them Ming and Ling! I have a new geography project and I need some help. I have to choose a country and write about the country and its people."

"Sounds like you are going to be busy tonight," Grandma commented.

Rose nodded and continued, "Camelia is going to write about Egypt because her father was born in Egypt and she has lots of relatives living in Egypt. Ruby is going to write about Vietnam because her parents immigrated to the USA from there, almost a year ago. Christina is going to write about Mexico because her parents were born in Mexico and immigrated to the USA before she was born. Fahd and Abdul are my new big brothers from Saudi Arabia, so I want Fahd and Abdul to help me write about Saudi Arabia!" Rose paused to catch her breath after her non-stop explanation.

"We will be most happy to help you, Little Sister," said Fahd. Abdul smiled and nodded his head in agreement.

Rose smiled back at Fahd and replied, "I need to get my project paper, a notepad, and some pencils."

"Let's go inside and sit at the dining room table. It will be easier for Rose to take notes sitting at the table, and I just finished cleaning it up from our gun cleaning mess," said Grandma.

Grandma, Fahd, and Abdul went inside to the dining room and sat down at the table to wait for Rose. Within minutes, Rose rushed into the dining room waving her notepad, pencils, and a piece of paper over her head.

"I'm ready now." Rose placed the notepad and pencils on the table and stood in front of Grandma and the boys as she held the paper out in front of her. She glanced at everyone to make sure they were paying attention. She saw three smiling faces staring back at her.

Rose paused a moment longer as she savored the attention. Rose was prone to be just a little dramatic, but always in a nice way.

"Any time now," Grandma said pleasantly enough. Rose knew from long experience, Grandma's tone of voice and those words really meant, "Stop delaying! Get finished! Hurry up!"

Rose quickly cleared her throat and began reading her assignment instructions out loud in a clear voice and at a slow pace so Fahd and Abdul would not have trouble understanding. They could really speak English well now and only had difficulty understanding if a person talked fast.

Within minutes, Rose finished reading, looked up from her instructions, and waited for Grandma or one of the boys to say something.

"I can help you draw a map of Saudi Arabia and put in the mountains, deserts, main cities, surrounding countries, and bodies of water that are on three boundaries of my country," Abdul offered.

Fahd said, "I will use your grandma's computer to go to our Embassy website. There we will find much information about my country. You can read the questions you must answer and I will look for them at the website. Anything we don't find, I am sure Abdul and I can tell you."

Grandma went to Rose's study-playroom and brought back the big map book. Grandma began looking for Middle Eastern countries. Abdul said he could use the map book to help him and Rose draw the map of Saudi Arabia.

For the next two hours, everyone worked on Rose's project. Rose wrote many notes from the information she and Fahd found at the website. The silence in the room was so comfortable that you could almost reach out and touch it. Finally, Grandma, Rose, Fahd, and Abdul put down their pencils and stretched.

Just then the strident ringing of the telephone broke the silence in the room.

Ring! Ring!

Ring! Ring!

Everyone jumped as their companionable silence was broken by the insistently ringing telephone. Grandma stretched again and said, "I guess I better go answer it." Fahd, Abdul, and Rose nodded and went back their daydreaming.

When Grandma returned to the dining room, she had a big smile on her face. "Your dad is ordering cheese pizza for supper. No cooking for me tonight!"

"Super!" squealed Rose. She loved cheese pizza!

Fahd and Abdul smiled at Rose's enthusiasm. "Sorry, Mum, but it is getting close to time for Maghrib prayer. We will eat some pizza when we return later this evening. Please thank Rose's dad for us," Abdul said as he and Fahd stood up and prepared to leave for the masjid.

"There will be plenty of pizza left, and I think Rose and I might make a green salad and whip up some of your favorite date nut bread to have with coffee and milk later on this evening," Grandma replied.

❧

After Fahd and Abdul left, Grandma got busy in the kitchen making the date nut bread. Rose wasn't going to be left out, because her favorite part of baking was licking the bowl, eggbeaters, and spatula! Just as Grandma placed the half-filled loaf pans into the oven to bake, Rose's dad opened the front door and yelled, "Pizza Delivery!"

Rose ran over to her dad and hugged him around his waist. "Yum! I'm so hungry I could eat a bear!" she exclaimed.

Tony chuckled and carried the two large boxes of pizza into the kitchen and placed them on the counter. "Hello, Mom," he said as he bent to kiss the top of Grandma's head. "How is my favorite girl today?"

"Hey!" Rose pretended to pout with her lower lip thrust out. "I thought I was your best girl!"

Rose's dad ruffled her hair, swung her up into the air, and, as he set her back down, he tickled her under her chin. "You are both my two best girls." Rose's dad laughed at her now smiling face as he carried a plateful of the pizza that Grandma had been cutting into the dining room.

"Rose, get the salad from the refrigerator, and I'll bring the salad bowls, forks, and some extra napkins," Grandma called over her shoulder as she followed her son into the dining room.

∾

"I am completely stuffed," said Rose as she licked pizza sauce from her fingers.

"You didn't eat much salad," Grandma admonished.

"I know," said Rose. "I ate too many pieces of pizza."

"I'm stuffed, too, and hate to eat and run, Mom, but I have another report to finish for work," Tony said as he began to gather together the used paper plates and dirty napkins.

"Just leave everything, Son. Rose and I can manage just fine. And thanks for the pizza!" Grandma called after her son as he headed for the front door.

Tony met Fahd and Abdul as he was leaving and they were returning from the masjid.

"See you later, Dad," Rose called out as she carried the dirty plates to the wastebasket.

"As-Salaam'Alaykum, Rose and Mum," the boys chorused as they hungrily eyed the pizza.

"Just wait a minute while I get some warm pizza from the oven, Boys," Grandma said as she headed for the kitchen. Rose carried some clean plates, salad bowls, forks, and napkins to the table for Fahd and Abdul and sat down next to Abdul. Grandma placed the hot pizza and the salad in the center of the table and returned to the kitchen.

Before Fahd or Abdul could even take one bite of their pizza, Rose gave a huge sigh to get their attention. "Remember when we were talking about names?" Rose asked with a very serious expression on her face.

Abdul and Fahd both nodded their heads and waited for Rose to continue.

"At school, some of the kids are mean to Ruby and call her 'slant eyes' and they were calling Camelia 'rag head' before we started to wear our Hijab-Ez scarves. These are not nice names!" Rose said vehemently. "There is one boy in another class who still calls Ruby 'slant eyes.' Christina wants to punch him in the nose."

Fahd and Abdul struggled to keep a straight face. Christina's first response was always a physical one.

"Camelia suggested we tell the teacher, but then if we do tell, all the other kids will start calling us snitches."

"What is snitches?" Fahd asked.

Grandma had been listening to the conversation. She came into the dining room, sat down, and explained to Fahd. "In our country, especially among young children, a child who points out another child's wrongdoing to a teacher or person in authority is called a snitch."

"But, this name of 'slant eyes' is hurtful. Is it not good to have this boy stop saying this? Why would children think this is bad to report this boy?" Abdul asked. This idea puzzled him.

"I do not understand this thinking," Fahd added.

"Not all children or people believe it is wrong, but there are many who do. Children don't want to be made fun of, and so they often do not speak up because they are afraid of the mean kids doing this kind of harmful name calling," replied Grandma.

Rose nodded her head and said, "That's why I asked what we should do."

"You would have a way to tell a teacher and she would not know who tells her?" Abdul asked.

Everyone was silent, thinking about what Abdul had just said.

"What about the suggestion box in the school office? You could write a note saying name calling should not be done at the school because it hurts kids," Grandma suggested.

"Oh, Grandma, that's a great idea! Should I put the names that kids say in this note?" Rose asked excitedly.

"Maybe you could say something about not making fun of kids because they look different, speak a different language, or might not have clothes that are the latest fad. This might be a better way to write your note," offered Grandma.

"Hmmm…maybe you could write it, Grandma. If I write it or the Hijab-Ez, some teacher might know our handwriting."

Grandma smiled at Rose. "Yes, I will write the note and I will put it in the suggestion box when I pick you up from school tomorrow."

Rose got up from the table, went to Grandma, and hugged her tight. "Thanks, Grandma. I can't wait to tell the Hijab-Ez tomorrow!"

"This is a good idea," Abdul said to Grandma.

Fahd smiled and nodded his head in agreement. "Little Sister, I am always thinking this. Why did Little Sister call her friend-group Hijab-Ez?"

Rose grinned when she heard Fahd's question. No one in her family had asked her why she made up the name. "The 'hijab' part of the name is because Camelia wears a hijab scarf. I read where hijab means covering. The 'Ez' part of the name is for the word 'easy.' Hijab-Ez means it is easy to cover! At first, I was kind of scared to wear a scarf like Camelia does every day. The Islam book of Grandma's said that Islam is a religion of ease, so I thought ease would go good with the hijab. I just spelled the word 'ease' like it sounds," Rose said with satisfaction.

Fahd and Abdul smiled approvingly at Rose, and Grandma chuckled. "Sometimes I just don't know where you come up with your ideas."

Rose grinned back at everyone and then her face took on her I-just-thought-of-something look.

"Are you going out with your friends tonight?"

"No. Tonight, Fahd and I are staying home. We have to leave very early tomorrow morning to drive to the firearms range."

Rose was happy because Fahd and Abdul would be home tonight. The wheels continued to churn, and her idea became clear as crystal in Rose's ever-busy mind. Without realizing it, Rose slowly rubbed her two hands together in anticipation. Grandma noticed Rose's gesture and shook her head. *I wonder what that minx is planning,* she thought.

"I asked my dad if I could stay for a while at your house, Grandma. Dad said I could, if it was okay with you. He said he'd call me when it's time to go home. Can I visit for awhile longer?" Rose asked sweetly. Maybe just a little too sweetly! Rose's face was the picture of innocence.

"Did you have something special in mind to do tonight?" Grandma asked, pretending she didn't suspect Rose had an idea waiting to spring upon them.

Fahd and Abdul had spied Rose's hand rubbing gestures and the whimsical expression on her face. They also knew from experience that Rose was planning something.

"I just thought that you grown-ups must be tired after a long day and you might want to relax. The best way to relax is to listen to a good story, and Fahd is the best storyteller in the room!"

Fahd, Grandma, and Abdul burst out laughing. Rose grinned at them sheepishly and joined in their laughter.

—— 6 ——

The Kitten Man

Rose rushed through the back door, yelling, "Grandma! Grandma!" *Where is everybody?* Rose looked in the family room and the living room, and didn't see anyone.

It was Sunday morning and a couple of weeks after Spring Break. Rose had been playing in Grandma's backyard for the past hour.

"Fahd, Abdul?" Rose continued through the house, calling out, "Anyone?" No one answered Rose.

Rose hurried to the front door and poked her head out. "Grandma, Fahd, Abdul! Where is everyone?" she yelled loudly.

Rose heard Grandma call out, "I'm cutting some of my roses. Is something wrong?"

Rose hurried to the side of the house and saw Grandma squatting in front of the "Peace" rosebush. Grandma looked so funny when she wore her gardening clothes. She had on an enormous red and white hat with a broad rim that dipped over her eyes, an old pair of Grandpa's faded jeans that had holes in each knee, a long-sleeved, checkered shirt that was at least three sizes too large for her, and flowered garden gloves. Grandma's long brown hair was braided and hung down her back. Pieces of twigs and leaves were stuck to the ends of the braid.

When Grandma smiled, her eyes would crinkle up at the corners and make them seem to almost disappear. She was smiling now at Rose as she tipped her hat back and got to her feet.

"Where are Fahd and Abdul? I have something important to show all of you. You are not going to believe it, even when you see it!" a breathless and excited Rose exclaimed.

Rose's eyes were dancing and a grin spread across her face causing her nose to wrinkle up and her eyes to crinkle in the corners just like Grandma's squinty eyes. Rose's long blonde hair was tied in a ponytail, and her bangs were so long they seemed to act like a broom swishing across the bridge of her freckled nose as she tossed her head back when she looked up at her Grandma.

"The boys went to the market for me and won't be back for an hour or so. Do you want to wait till they get home or can I see what I won't believe?" asked Grandma as she grinned back at Rose.

Rose grabbed Grandma's hand saying, "Come on and hurry up, Grandma. You're going to be sooo surprised!"

Rose and Grandma hurried through the house and out the back door to the patio. Rose held her finger up to her lips and whispered, "Shish, don't say anything." Rose guided Grandma to the laundry room door, which was slightly ajar. With an impish smile, Rose carefully opened the door wider and pointed to a cardboard box in a dark corner next to Grandpa's toolbox.

Grandma and Rose tiptoed quietly into the room and slowly made their way to the cardboard box. Rose hung back just a few steps and watched Grandma bend over to peek inside the box.

Grandma exclaimed and quickly clamped her hand over her mouth. Grandma took a quick count, "One and two, three, four, five?" Inside the box, on a tattered old blanket, were five tiny fur balls. Grandma felt something brush against her pant legs and watched in amazement as Taffy, Rose's cat, jumped into the box and began licking each of the fur balls.

"Five!" squealed Rose as she tugged on Grandma's right arm. Rose nudged Grandma and bent over the box. "One, two, three, four and five," she counted out loud. There had been only three fur balls when Rose went searching for Grandma earlier.

"I thought Taffy was a he," giggled Rose.

"Me, too," laughed Grandma as she reached in and scratched one of Taffy's ears.

"Just wait until Grandpa, Fahd, and Abdul see them. They won't believe it!" Rose whispered as the five fur balls began to squirm and mew.

"Can I pick one of them up and hold it?" questioned Rose.

"The kittens are much too small to handle right now. We don't want Taffy to get anxious and hide them do we?" Grandma answered and patted the top of Rose's head fondly.

"No, I guess not. When can I hold one?" Rose stuck out a finger and gently rubbed Taffy's paw.

"Not for at least a week or two. We have to let Taffy and the kittens rest and get used to each other," said Grandma.

Rose gazed in wonder at the newborn kittens. One kitten was all black, another was black with white ears, and a third was a yellowish-tan color, the same as Taffy. The fourth kitten was all white. The fifth and smallest of the five kittens was black, yellow, white, tan, and gray.

"Look, Grandma, the smallest kitten has a coat-of-many-colors," Rose whispered excitedly. "Can we keep them, all of them?" she pleaded.

Grandma gently pulled on Rose's sleeve and pointed to the laundry room door. Rose gave one last longing look at the five fur balls and followed Grandma. Once outside, Grandma and Rose sat down in the glider, and Rose waited anxiously to hear if they would keep the kittens.

"Rose, you already have three cats and a dog..." began Grandma.

"I know, I know, but, but..." Rose sputtered trying to think of a good reason to keep all five kittens.

Grandma took Rose's chin in her hands and tilted Rose's head upward so she could look directly at Rose. "You may choose one kitten to keep, but we will have to find homes for the other four when they are big enough to get along without Taffy." Grandma's tone of voice was firm, but kind. Rose knew that pleading would not change Grandma's mind. She was disappointed, but already knew how much cat food and shots and stuff like that cost for her other three cat friends. *Okay*, she thought. *I need a PLAN and I need help!*

Grandma didn't want Rose to sit around all afternoon and brood about the kittens so she said, "Who wants to help me make cookies?"

A smile lit up Rose's face. She hugged Grandma and said, "I do!"

Grandma and Rose went into the kitchen. "I'll read the recipe to you, and you can get the ingredients." Rose nodded her head as she went to the sink to wash her hands. Grandma went to get the recipe book.

"How about making some Double Whammy Choco Bars?" Grandma read the name from a list of cookies in the recipe book index.

"No. Wait a minute. I know the recipe I like the best." Rose took the book and turned to a dog-eared page that was covered with grease stains and had a smear of leftover cookie dough stuck on it. "Let's make Chocolate Filled Thumbprint Cookies," suggested Rose. Grandma smacked her lips and agreed.

Now, Grandma was renowned among her children, grandchildren, and anyone who visited her for her yummy in the tummy cookies! Chocolate cookies were her specialty. Rose and Grandma got busy. Cookie making was one of their favorite fun things to do, especially on a lazy Sunday afternoon.

Several hours later, Rose was blissfully munching a freshly baked cookie and drinking an oversized glass of milk. She hadn't stopped thinking about the problem of the kittens for very long, though.

All too soon, Rose broached the subject of the kittens again. "Who will we give the kittens to? How will we know if the people will be kind and feed them right? How soon will we have to give them away?" Rose looked earnestly at Grandma and waited for her to reply.

"The kittens will be able to go to their new homes in about six weeks. I think we can come up with an idea on how to find them homes by then," Grandma replied.

"Can I call Camelia and tell her about the new kittens? Maybe she will have some good ideas." Grandma nodded her head as she chewed the last bite of her cookie. Rose hurried to the living room and telephoned Camelia.

A minute later, Rose returned to the kitchen. The corners of her mouth were turned down and her lips looked like an upside down bowl. "Camelia not at home?" asked Grandma.

"No, and I tried Ruby and Christina, too. Nobody is at home, but me," Rose said dejectedly.

"You can cheer up, my sweetie pie. Tomorrow will come soon enough, and you can tell your friends at school. You will have a nice surprise for them." Grandma gave Rose a quick hug. "I think I hear a car in the driveway."

Dad and Grandpa were expected home from work any time now. The front door opened, and Dad and Grandpa both stood in the doorway waiting for Rose to reach them. Rose hugged both of them, grabbed a hand of each, and said, "Come on and see the new kittens!"

Rose saw the peculiar looks that Dad and Grandpa gave each other. "I know what that look means," sniffed Rose. "Grandma said I can keep one kitten, and I am going to make a plan to find good homes for the other four."

"Four!" Grandpa and Dad said loudly at the same time. Grandma waved at Dad and Grandpa, and put her finger to her lips. "Quiet," her eyes said. Dad and Grandpa followed Rose out to the laundry room to see the new kittens.

Fahd and Abdul got home with the groceries just as Rose, Dad, and Grandpa came into the family room from seeing the new kittens. Rose took Fahd and Abdul out to see the new kittens. She was so excited she seemed to be bubbling like a pot of Grandma's stew! Dashing in and out from the laundry room, Rose was soon out of breath.

"Time for us to go home now, Rose. You can help me fix supper and then early to bed for you. Tomorrow is a school day."

"Okay, Dad. I just want to get my journal and I'll be right over." Rose smiled at everyone and hurried to her study-playroom to retrieve the journal she had named Jammie last summer when she was so lonesome and didn't have any friends to play with. Rose had lots to "tell" Jammie, especially about the new kittens!

❧

Monday morning, Rose was rushing around her house getting her schoolbooks together and looking for her handkerchief scarf. "Did you lose something?" asked Dad.

"Oh, fudge! I think I left my scarf at Grandma's." Rose hugged her Dad, said goodbye, and hurried across the front lawn to her grandma's house. Grandpa was just coming out the front door and he held out the scarf to Rose. "Thanks, Grandpa. I can't be a Hijab-Ez without my head scarf!"

Grandpa gently steered Rose towards the truck and said, "No time to check on the kittens. I'll do it for you when I get back home."

The scowl immediately cleared from Rose's face. "Thanks, Grandpa, you're a lifesaver!"

Minutes later, Grandpa pulled his truck into the school parking lot and kissed Rose goodbye. "Have a good day, Rose."

Rose gave her Grandpa a big hug and grabbed her book bag. *Oh, no!* Rose thought. *I'm late!*

Rose saw her Hijab-Ez friends waving to her. She rushed to get in line before the last bell rang.

"You're late!" whispered Camelia.

"I know. I was looking for my scarf all over the house and finally remembered I left it at my grandma's house. My grandpa didn't forget it."

"I was at Islamic school yesterday when you called me," whispered Camelia. "What was so important?"

"I've got a secret. I've got a secret!" giggled Rose.

"Shish!" Mrs. Rodriguez looked at Camelia and Rose, and frowned. "No talking in line!" Mrs. Rodriguez looked pointedly again at Rose and Camelia. Camelia's face turned beet red. Rose bowed her head and compressed her lips.

Ruby and Christina, the other two members of the Hijab-Ez friendship group, were standing behind Rose in the line. Christina pulled on the back of Rose's shirt. Rose turned sideways and saw Christina make a big question mark with her finger in the air. Rose shook her head and turned around to see Mrs. Rodriguez watching her. *Oh boy! First I'm late, now Mrs. Rodriguez isn't happy with me, and the day has just started!*

～

Finally, the lunch bell rang, and Rose and her friends hurried to get in line for the cafeteria. As soon as they sat down at their usual table and spread their lunches out to share with each other, Christina looked at Rose and Camelia, and said, "So, what is going on?"

"What were you whispering about this morning?" chimed in Ruby.

Ruby, Christina, and Camelia sat silently and looked expectantly at Rose. Rose smirked at them and waited to answer, savoring up to the last minute sharing her surprise.

"Well, if you are just going to sit there like a bump on a log, I'm going to eat," an indignant Ruby sputtered. Ruby took eating lunch very seriously.

"Okay! Okay, already! My cat Taffy had five new kittens yesterday!" Rose enjoyed watching the delighted and then questioning looks on her friends' faces.

"But...but, I thought Taffy was a boy!" Christina exclaimed.

"We were wrong." Rose's voice squeaked and she continued, "There's something else. My grandma says I can keep only one of the new kittens. I have six weeks to find good homes for the rest of the kittens."

"We need a PLAN!" Camelia said in a very positive voice.

"Now you sound just like Rose," giggled Christina. "Maybe you could sell them!?"

"Or I could have a raffle if enough kids want a kitten," said Rose.

"No raffles! Muslims don't participate in raffles, play the lottery, or gamble. It's like riba," Camelia said firmly.

"Riba, what's riba?" Christina asked.

"My father said that riba is charging someone interest when you loan them money. You are not supposed to benefit because someone needs a loan. You are not supposed to charge someone to help them. Raffles and lotteries are like gambling. You pay a little and hope to get back more than you paid. Muslims don't think this is an honest way to treat people."

"Oh," was all Christina said. She wasn't sure if she understood this riba, but for sure the raffle idea was O-U-T, out!

Suddenly it dawned on Rose, Christina, and Camelia that Ruby hadn't said anything. She just kept eating her lunch and their lunch too!

"Will you stop eating long enough to help us out? Rose has a real problem, and we need to help her," Camelia said with just a hint of exasperation.

Ruby very deliberately put down her half-eaten dill pickle and said, "I've been thinking while you three have been talking."

Christina rolled her eyes and poked Rose in the side. "Our brain has been thinking. Do you have any ideas?"

"We should have an 'Adopt a Kitty Contest'," Ruby calmly stated. She wasn't upset at Christina's teasing. "We could post pictures of the kittens in our classroom, and our classmates can fill in an application to adopt a kitten."

"Super-de-duper idea!" Rose clapped her hands. "I think it would work!" Rose pulled out her notepad and pencil, and began writing notes. "I'll ask Grandpa to take a picture of each kitten when they are about two weeks old."

"I can make some posters," offered Ruby. They all agreed that Ruby was a fantastic artist and the best Hijab-Ez for this task.

"Christina and I can write the application questions. We can give them to the students who are interested in adopting a kitten," said Camelia.

Rose smiled at her friends. She had known they would come through for her. They were the best friends ever! "Wait a minute!

What if more than four students make out an application?" Rose looked at her friends and they all fell silent pondering this new wrinkle to their fabulous PLAN.

"After we get the applications, we could pick the four that are the best ones to get a kitten. We would be the selection committee." Ruby looked at her friends to see what they thought about this idea.

"It sounds good to me," Christina said.

"Me, too," chimed in Rose.

Camelia didn't say anything.

Rose, Ruby, and Christina looked at Camelia. "Now, what's the problem?" Rose asked.

"I think we need some kind of rules or reasons for selecting the students who get a kitten." Camelia looked thoughtfully at her three friends. "Did I ever tell you the 'Kitten Man' story?"

Rose's eyes gleamed. She just loved hearing stories, especially stories that had anything at all about cats or kittens in the story. "No, and I would have remembered if you had told us this story."

"We want to hear the story," chorused Ruby and Christina.

"I think the story is gonna help us make some rules," grinned Rose with a knowing look at Camelia. Camelia smiled back and began her story.

"Many, many years ago in the land of Arabia, there lived a poor man named *Abdu-Shams*. His name means 'Servant of the Sun.' The chief of his tribe became a Muslim, and Abdu-Shams wanted to know why he had done this. His chief told him about Prophet Muhammad (pbuh). Abdu-Shams decided to go to Mecca, where the Prophet lived, and meet him. When the Prophet (pbuh) met with Abdu-Shams, he asked Abdu-Shams, 'What is your name? When the Prophet (pbuh) heard what his name was, he told Abdu-Shams to change his name to *Abdur-Rahman*, which means 'Servant of the Merciful.' The Prophet (pbuh) didn't believe in worshipping idols. Some people worshipped the sun back in ancient days!

"Abdur-Rahman liked his new name and he liked being with the Prophet, so he stayed with him. Soon, everyone noticed how kind Abdur-Rahman was to every animal. He always had a cat or kitten with him and he loved to play with them. The Prophet noticed him playing with the cats and kittens and called out, 'O Abu Hurairah. This nickname means 'Cat Father' or 'Kitten Man'."

Camelia looked across the table at Rose and smiled at her. Rose's eyes glittered from pure happiness and her grin seemed to stretch from ear to ear.

"Is there more to your story?" Rose asked excitedly.

"Now comes the best part," said Camelia and continued with the story.

"Abu Hurairah became a Muslim and traveled everywhere with the Prophet (pbuh). One night, he was praying in the masjid, and the Prophet (pbuh) overheard him ask Allah for knowledge that would not be forgotten. From that night until he died, Abu Hurairah remembered all the sayings of the Prophet (pbuh). People began saying, 'Ask Abu Hurairah,' if they were not sure what the Prophet (pbuh) said. Today, Muslims quote the sayings of the Prophet (pbuh) as reported by Abu Hurairah.

"Abu Hurairah was never selfish. He was poor and an orphan from the time he was very young. He loved the Prophet (pbuh) so much that often he would go hungry when they didn't have much food to eat. He traveled with the Prophet (pbuh) almost four years and carried his favorite cat with him during the whole time!"

Camelia looked at her friends, and each one of them thanked her for the story. "That was a super story, Camelia, but how does it help us decide on our selection rules?" Christina was puzzled and wondered if she had missed something important. No one answered.

Rose was busy writing in her notepad. She looked up from her writing when she noticed no one was talking.

"What are you writing?" asked Ruby.

"I'm making a list of all the things about the 'Kitten Man' that made him so special. I think Camelia and Christina can use the list to help them make the questions for the application paper, and we can use the list to help us pick the people that get

Linda D. Delgado

to adopt the kittens." Rose handed the newly written list to
Christina. Christina read the list out loud.

Kitten Man's special qualities include:

Kind—will be gentle with the kitten
Merciful—not mean
Loyal—will not let anyone hurt the kitten
Caring—will brush kitten and get shots for kitten
Unselfish—will remember to look out for kitten
Smart—will learn how to care for kitten
Curious—fun
Loves God—will love the kitten
Good memory—will remember to feed the kitten
Playful—will play with the kitten
Note—one point for each quality an applicant has.

"That's a good list. I think we need the kids to get their
parents to sign the application agreeing to take the kitten,"
Camelia added.

Rose picked up the list and added Camelia's suggestion. "Do
we have a PLAN or do we have a S-U-P-E-R, super PLAN!?"
Rose bubbled.

They looked at Ruby. Slowly, Ruby began to smile and soon
her smile spread to each of her friends. The four girls held up
their pinkie fingers and softly said in unison, "Hijab–Ez! Friends
forever!"

❧

When Grandma and Rose got home from school that
afternoon, Rose told her about the PLAN the girls had made at
lunch time. Rose also told Grandma about the story of Abu
Hurairah, the 'Kitten Man.'

"What a wonderful story! Now you have a story to tell Fahd,"
laughed Grandma. Grandma suggested that the applications have
a place for a phone number. She said she would call the parents

114

to make sure they wanted a kitten. Grandma told Rose that Grandpa would take the kittens to the school when the kittens were old enough to be given to their new owners.

Rose went out to the laundry room to sneak a peek at the new kittens. She spoke quietly to the kittens and to Taffy. "I promise, my friends, I will find each of you a good home." When Rose came back inside, she said to Grandma, "I have decided to keep the kitten with the coat-of-many-colors."

"Have you decided on a name for your newest cat friend?" Grandma had known Rose would pick this kitten. Grandma always seemed to know the things that were important to Rose.

Rose smiled at her grandma and said, "I think I am going to name my new kitten *Abu*!"

7

The Peace Maker

"TGIF! Thank God It's Friday," Christina mumbled as she chewed on a stalk of celery. She stared at Ruby sitting across from her at their lunch table. Ruby was chomping her way through almost everything spread out in the center of the table. "Slow down, Ruby, maybe the rest of us want to eat, too!" Christina chided her friend.

Ruby paused and was about to answer Christina when she noticed that Rose and Camelia weren't eating. Rose was sitting with her elbows on the table, chin resting in her hands, and staring off into space. Camelia was sitting next to Ruby with her head bowed and twisting a piece of paper held in her hands.

Ruby looked back at Christina and mouthed silently, "What's wrong?" She pointed at their two silent friends.

Christina looked at Rose and Camelia, then back at Ruby, and shrugged her shoulders. A deep frown began to furrow Christina's forehead.

Ruby tried to get Rose's attention by tossing a piece of apple at the milk carton sitting in front of Rose. Rose didn't blink an eye. Christina threw a second piece of apple at the milk carton. Rose just sat there. Camelia looked up, stared at the piece of apple, and heaved a big sigh.

"What is with the two of you?" Christina nearly shouted. "You are not eating and you both look like the end of the world is about to start!" Rose and Camelia didn't answer Christina.

Ruby wondered if Rose was sad about the kittens. Before school started, Rose's grandpa had brought the four kittens to the school, and the kittens were given to the parents of the winners of the 'Adopt a Kitten Contest.' Rose had acted really happy because they had found good homes for each of the kittens. Practically the whole school had crowded onto the school parking lot that morning. Rose, Ruby, Christina, and Camelia had each carried a small kitten to its new owner. Grandpa had taken pictures, and everyone had applauded. Even Mr. Stein, the principal, had come out to watch the kitten transfer ceremony!

Maybe Rose is worrying about how the other kids will take care of the kittens. But, Camelia looks so upset. She's twisting that paper and she looks like she is going to cry! I wonder what is bothering her. It can't be the same thing that's bothering Rose, Ruby thought as she looked at her sad friends.

Christina noticed Camelia twisting the paper and asked, "Why are you twisting that paper Camelia? It looks like you are trying to be a human shredding machine!" No one laughed at Christina's attempt to lighten the mood around the table with her little joke.

Ruby couldn't stand it anymore. She grabbed the crumpled paper from Camelia and began smoothing out the wrinkles. Christina thought, *Oh boy! There is something seriously wrong happening here! Camelia didn't protest when Ruby grabbed the paper from her hands.*

Rose suddenly slammed her hands down on the table and muttered loudly, "It's not fair!"

"What's not fair?" Christina squeaked nervously as she looked at a now angry faced Rose.

"I'm so mad I could bite nails!" Ruby nearly shouted in an angry voice. Her three friends all looked at Ruby with shocked expressions on their faces. Ruby almost never raised her voice and never, ever got mad!

"Shish," whispered Camelia. "Everyone is looking at us!"

Ruby's face reddened and she whispered back, "Well, Rose is right. It's not fair!"

"Will somebody puh-lease tell me what is going on?!" Christina wailed.

"Shish!" whispered Camelia again. Christina noticed a small tear trickle slowly down Camelia's cheek.

Ruby slid the crumpled paper across the table to Christina and said, "Read that and don't yell. The lunchroom monitor is giving us some ugly looks right now."

"I'm going to start a protest, make signs, and picket the school office," Rose exclaimed rebelliously. Rose jutted out her chin, scrunched up her eyes, and balled her small hands into fists.

"What!" Christina shouted.

"We're done for! Here comes Mrs. Bonner, the lunchroom monitor!" Ruby sputtered as she grabbed the wrinkled paper from Christina and quickly stuffed it into her lunch pail.

"*Ya Allah!*" exclaimed Camelia, distress written clearly across her sad face.

"Is something wrong, ladies?" Mrs. Bonner questioned the girls sarcastically as she looked at each of them with narrowed eyes, suspicion dripping from each word.

With an apologetic smile for Mrs. Bonner, Rose said sweetly, "We are sorry for making so much noise. We promise to be quiet."

Mrs. Bonner looked at each girl, and then replied, "Well, okay, young ladies, but if I hear one more raised voice, I will report your conduct to your teacher." With that said, Mrs. Bonner walked away leaving the four girls gasping with relief.

"*Subhanahu wa ta'ala* (Glory be to Him the Almighty)," breathed Camelia.

Very quietly her three friends said, "That goes for me, too."

The bell rang for class to begin. Rose and her friends hurried out of the lunchroom. One more hour, and then school would be over for the day. Rose whispered to her friends that they would talk about Camelia's problem when they got to her grandma's house after school. Rose had invited her friends to spend Friday afternoon at her grandma's house so they could practice reciting the poems they had entered in the school's annual poetry contest. Winners would compete in the school district and then statewide.

Next Monday, contestants had to recite their original poem in front of the entire school body. Rose and her friends had entered the contest and they needed to practice reciting their poems. Camelia looked at Rose, and then quickly looked away.

"You are coming and no excuses!" Rose stated firmly to her friend. Camelia nodded okay as they entered their classroom.

Grandma sat in her car, parked in the school parking lot, and watched as four solemn-faced young girls approached. Rose and her three friends stopped, suddenly. Ruby, then Rose, and finally Christina hugged Camelia. All four girls raised their right hands in the air, extended their pinkie finger, and yelled, "Hijab-Ez! Friends forever!"

"Uh-oh," exclaimed Grandma out loud. *Something has happened and the Hijab-Ez are gearing up to tackle a problem!* Rose broke away from her friends and hurried to reach Grandma first. She handed Grandma a crumpled sheet of paper and demanded, "Read it!" Rose opened the back door of the car as her friends approached, and everyone climbed in.

Grandma read the paper and sighed heavily. She put the crumpled sheet of paper on the seat next to her and turned to Camelia. "I am so very sorry this has happened, sweetheart. When we get to my house, I will telephone your mother and ask her to come over so we can talk about this."

Camelia gave Grandma a wobbly smile. "Thanks, I really want to see my mother right away."

When they got to Grandma's house, Camelia went to the restroom to get ready for Friday Jumu'ah prayer. Grandma told Camelia to use the back bedroom to say her prayer and added that Fahd had placed a prayer rug in the direction of the Ka'bah for her. "I will call your mother as soon as prayer time is finished."

Rose got each of her friends a bottle of juice, and they went to the family room to wait for Camelia. When Camelia rejoined her friends, Grandma picked up the telephone and called

Camelia's mother. After only a minute, Grandma came into the family room.

"Your mother is on her way here, Camelia, and she said to give you a big hug!" Grandma hugged Camelia and patted her cheek. "We will work this out. You didn't do anything wrong. Remember that, okay?"

Camelia smiled at Rose's grandma. Already she felt better after saying her prayer. She had asked Allah to help her get over her anger and hurt.

"Maybe this is all just a big mistake," offered Ruby. "The teacher is from another school and he doesn't know you, Camelia. I wonder if our principal knows about this."

The Hijab-Ez discussed the situation for the next ten minutes or so.

The doorbell rang, and Camelia ran to the door. Grandma quickly followed her and opened the door. "As-Salaam'Alaykum," Grandma greeted Camelia's mother, Judy.

"Wa'alaykum as-Salaam," replied Judy as she wrapped her arms around Camelia. "Thank you for calling me and inviting me to your home. Where is the paper?"

They walked into the family room, and Rose handed Judy the wrinkled sheet of paper. Judy sat in Grandpa's easy chair with Camelia seated on her lap. Rose, Ruby, and Christina sat on the floor, while Grandma sat down on the couch. They all waited silently as Judy read the paper.

When Judy finished reading, she gave Camelia a big squeeze and kissed her. "Honey, I need to talk to your father about this. I am sure he will give us some good advice. You did not make any mistakes. I think the teacher who wrote these comments has made the mistakes."

Rose wasn't so calm about what had happened to her best friend and she said with conviction, "I think we should hold a rally, make protest signs, and picket the school office!"

"I think we should just boycott the whole thing!" exclaimed Ruby.

"I didn't want to do it anyway," grumbled Christina. "Now I know why I don't like contests!"

"Let's not be so hasty, girls," cautioned Grandma. "We need to give Camelia and her parents time to decide what they want to do about this situation first."

"I think Camelia and I need to go to the restaurant and talk with her father. He should have returned to the restaurant from Jumu'ah prayer by now. Thank you for your kindness, Linda. And thank you, girls, for your loyalty to Camelia." Judy smiled at Ruby, Rose, and Christina.

Camelia tugged on the sleeve of her mother's abaya. "Mom, I don't understand why the teacher said my poem was disqualified because it wasn't written in English. Isn't 'Allah' the English spelling for the word 'God'?"

Camelia had written an original poem about peace and entered the poem in the school's annual poetry contest. In Camelia's poem, she explained that the words "As-Salaam'Alaykum" mean "peace be on you." The teacher who reviewed every poem to ensure they met contest guidelines had circled on Camelia's poem the words "Allah" and "As-Salaam'Alaykum" with a red marker. At the bottom of the page, he wrote, "Your poem cannot be submitted to the panel of judges. You cannot recite your poem on Monday because you did not follow contest rules and use English only in your poem."

"Why did this teacher wait till today to return Camelia's poem? If he had given it back right away, maybe she could have changed the Arabic words to English!" Rose exclaimed indignantly.

"We don't know why the teacher reasoned this way," replied Grandma.

Ruby, always the thoughtful one of the Hijab-Ez, said quietly, "Camelia's poem is beautiful just like it is. Those words are needed to convey what Camelia feels about peace."

"Before you leave, would you recite your beautiful poem for us?" asked Grandma.

Camelia looked pleased when she heard Grandma's request and quickly nodded her head. She smoothed out the wrinkled paper and stood up in front of her mother, Grandma, and her friends. As she faced them, the shadows that had been chasing themselves across her face disappeared, and a warm smile spread, tilting the corners of her mouth upward. Her voice quavered and shook as she began to recite her poem, but grew strong and firm as she dropped the paper and spoke the words from her heart.

Hope for Peace

When I watch the nightly news
It makes me want to cry.
Kidnappings, hate crimes, this talk of war
And so many people who've violently died.
I ask why these terrible things happen.
Some say it's the environment raised in,
Some say it's just in the genes.
I say it's a lack of respect all around
That causes such evil to breed.
In school, we have many races.
There're kids Christian, Muslim and Jew
Yet we all work and play well together.
Why aren't adults able to do this, too?
Allah created our wonderful world
In it, nature's diversity is plain
So why can't we celebrate the beauty of our differences?
Instead of making them excuses to cause suffering and pain?
As for me, I'll bid you all As-Salaamu'Alaykum
And hope that this is something the entire world will see.
For the Muslims, this is a farewell and a greeting
Meaning, "peace upon you be."

When Camelia finished reciting, the family room erupted in loud applause! Camelia smiled impishly and nodded her head. She ran to her mother and hugged her. "My poem is nice, isn't it?"

Judy exclaimed, "Alhamdulillah (All praise be to Allah)!"

"It is a wonderful poem. It came from your heart," Rose said quietly. Already, Rose was thinking about what she would do on Monday, if Camelia's parents did not get the school to accept Camelia's poem.

"Time to go, Camelia," Judy smiled at the girls again, picked up Camelia's book bag, and began walking towards the front door. The four girls stood together in a huddle and hugged one another.

Christina handed Camelia the wrinkled paper that had been lying on the floor.

"Please call and let us know what your husband wants to do about this situation," Grandma said to Judy as she walked Camelia and Judy out to their car.

~

After Camelia and her mother left, Grandma listened to Rose, Ruby, and Christina practice reciting their poems. Each of the girls recited their poem twice. When Rose stood up the third time, she looked over at Grandma. "Can we quit for the day? I really don't feel like doing this anymore."

Grandma looked at the girls. They weren't smiling and their voices were subdued when they recited. "I think we've had enough of poetry for one day. I'll call your parents and tell them I'm bringing you home early."

Rose, Ruby, and Christina went to the back patio to see Rose's cat friends and meet Abu, Rose's new, coat-of-many-colors kitten. A few minutes later, Grandma called out to them that it was time to leave.

"What do you think Camelia's parents can do before Monday?" Ruby asked Rose as they climbed into the backseat of Grandma's car.

"Maybe the principal will overrule this teacher, if they asked him to do that," Christina chimed in.

"If Camelia can't recite her poem, then I have a PLAN that will make her feel better," Rose stated with a determined look towards her two friends.

Ruby and Christina looked at each other. When Rose got that look in her eyes, used that tone of voice, *and* said the word PLAN, they knew that something wonderful or a boatload of trouble was headed their way.

Grandma drove her car into the driveway just as Fahd and Abdul were coming out the front door of her house. She and Rose had just taken Ruby and Christina home. Rose got out of the car and greeted the boys with, "As-Salaam'Alaykum. Where are you going?"

The boys greeted Rose and Grandma and said they were going to The Phoenician Restaurant.

"Can I go with you, please?" wheedled Rose with an engaging smile for each of them.

"Rose!" Grandma said rather sharply. "Mind your manners!"

"It is okay, Mum. We are going to get supper and bring it home. Little Sister may come with us, if this is agreeable with you." Abdul laughed at Rose's woebegone look.

"All right," agreed Grandma and she laughed, too, when she saw Rose's face. Rose looked like she had eaten sour grapes! Rose's sour look changed to a grin when Grandma said she could go with the boys. She ran back to Grandma and gave her a hug and a thank-you.

"Would you like to go with us, Mum?" Abdul asked politely.

"No, thanks. I have had a busy afternoon and I am going to go inside and do some quiet reading." Grandma waved goodbye as Abdul's car backed out of the driveway and drove away.

"Whew! I sure am glad Grandma decided not to come with us. I have a problem and I need your help," Rose gushed out as soon as the car left the driveway.

In Rose's typical manner, she outlined the poetry contest and the teacher's rejection of Camelia's poem. Rose pulled a copy of Camelia's poem from her pocket and handed it to Fahd. Fahd read the poem out loud because Abdul was doing the driving. Seeing that Fahd had finished reading the poem, Rose declared that she was going to protest the poetry contest by getting the kids at school to join her in a boycott.

"Boycott?" Fahd questioned, with eyebrows raised and a confused look at Rose.

Rose explained to Fahd and Abdul that a boycott meant organizing the other children at school to disrupt the contest on Monday morning. Rose told them she planned to make signs and have the kids picket in front of the school office. She added she had seen people protesting on television and this was how she planned to get the school to treat Camelia fairly.

Rose looked at Fahd and he wasn't smiling. In fact, his frown had deepened.

Abdul pulled into the parking lot of The Phoenician Restaurant and parked his car. He turned to Rose and said, "I think our Little Sister is very angry right now. You are very loyal to your little friend, Camelia. This is good, but your anger is not so good."

"But, what do you mean?" Rose sputtered. She thought she would have the full support of Fahd and Abdul. They didn't seem to like her boycott idea.

"I want to tell you a story. It won't be a long story like Fahd tells, but I think it will help you see what I mean about your anger." Abdul smiled gently at Rose to take the sting out of his words.

Rose continued to wear a belligerent look, but the deep frown in her forehead eased, and she settled back into the cushion of the car's back seat to listen to Abdul's story. Abdul hardly ever told stories. This novelty had caught her attention!

Abdul began, "Before Prophet Muhammad (peace and blessings be upon him) became a prophet, he was a young man and he lived in Mecca. Remember Fahd told you in a story how Mecca grew around the Ka'bah?"

Rose nodded her head.

"After many years, traders from many lands forgot about Allah and put their idols in the Ka'bah. The leaders of Mecca liked this because it brought a lot of trade and people to Mecca each year.

"One year, there was a flood and all the water caused so much damage to the Ka'bah that it had to be rebuilt. The leaders of Mecca decided to have young men from many tribes help with rebuilding the Ka'bah. They were trying to avoid the different tribes fighting for this honor. There was a special stone called the *Hajri Aswad*, which means 'black stone,' that was part of the first Ka'bah Prophet Abraham built.

"When the Ka'bah was almost finished, all that was left to do was place this black stone inside it. The men from the different tribes began to argue. Each tribe wanted the honor of putting the black stone inside the Ka'bah. They were ready to fight, even go to war, when an old and wise leader of Mecca, *Abu Ummayah*, suggested they let the first man to walk into their group decide who should put the black stone inside the Ka'bah. The first man the group saw was Al-Ameen, which means 'The Trustworthy One'."

"I know who Al-Ameen is. He's Muhammad!" Rose exclaimed.

Fahd grinned and told Rose she was right.

"What did Muhammad do?" By this time Rose had forgotten her anger and was totally wrapped up in the story Abdul was telling her.

"He told the men to get a blanket and place the black stone in the center of it. Then a young man was chosen from each tribe to help carry the black stone inside the Ka'bah. Once inside the Ka'bah, Muhammad (pbuh) took the black stone and put it in its special place. Everyone cheered and was so relieved that Muhammad (pbuh) had stopped a war."

Abdul finished his story and asked Rose, "How did Muhammad (pbuh) stop the men from being angry and avert a war? What did he use?"

Rose sat quietly, thinking about the story. Abdul didn't want her to tell him what Muhammad had done; he wanted to know how Muhammad had done it. *Hmm…*Rose thought.

Fahd and Abdul sat quietly and let Rose think about the story.

Rose began with, "Muhammad didn't show any anger and he was calm. He made a plan, but his plan was a peaceful one."

"Yes, Little Sister. You are correct." Abdul smiled. Fahd nodded his head approvingly and smiled at Rose, too.

"Then I need to make a peaceful plan that will help Camelia stop feeling hurt. I also want the school leaders to know that their decision about Camelia's poem is unfair and wrong." Rose looked questioningly at Abdul and Fahd, and they nodded and smiled back at her.

"I will spend more time thinking about a peaceful PLAN to help Camelia." Rose felt the butterflies in her stomach disappear, and a sense of quiet determination filled her heart.

"Now, let's go inside and get some supper. My stomach wants food, now!" Fahd's eyes grew wide and he made a silly face.

"Your grandma will think we are lost," joked Fahd. Rose began to giggle and suddenly she was hungry, too!

When they got home, Grandma told them the sad news. Camelia's mother had called her and explained that they had not been able to reach the principal. He was gone for the weekend and wouldn't be available until Monday morning. Monday would be too late to help Camelia before the poetry recital. Grandma told Rose that Camelia had decided to go to school on Monday anyway to support Rose and her other friends when they recited their own poems.

While they ate their supper, Rose's mind churned and wheels turned. *I need a peaceful plan*, Rose thought. *Please God help me to help my friend*, Rose prayed silently. Grandma, Fahd, and Abdul stole looks at Rose as she sat with her spoon hovering over her bowl of soup. Rose sat motionless, her thoughts far away in the PLAN just taking root in her mind. Suddenly, a slow smile appeared to grow on her face. Grandma and the boys nodded to each other and smiled. They knew Rose had found a solution for a peaceful PLAN.

After supper, Rose, Abdul, and Fahd went out to the back patio while Grandma cleaned up the dirty dishes and kitchen. Rose told the boys her PLAN, and they promised to help her. Rose, Abdul, and Fahd worked all weekend on the PLAN.

◆

Monday morning, Rose, Dad, Grandma, Grandpa, Fahd, and Abdul arrived at the school in time to meet Camelia and her parents. Christina, Ruby, and their families also joined them. Camelia went with the grownups to find a seat in the school auditorium, while Rose, Ruby, and Christina joined the other poetry contestants behind the stage. Rose saw her teacher, Mrs. Rodriguez. She went to her and whispered in her ear. Mrs. Rodriguez nodded her head. Rose walked back to the line of students with a satisfied smile on her lips. Christina and Ruby asked Rose what she had whispered to Mrs. Rodriguez.

"I asked her if I could be the last contestant." Rose smiled secretively at Ruby and Christina. She then told them her peaceful PLAN.

Ruby and Christina gasped when Rose finished talking. "Are you sure you want to do that?" whispered Ruby.

"I think it's a great PLAN," exclaimed Christina. "Can I stand on the stage with you?"

After only a small hesitation, Ruby chimed in, "Me, too?"

"I knew I could count on both of you," an elated Rose grinned.

Rose peeked through the stage curtains and saw Grandpa holding the movie camera while standing near the front row on the right side of the stage. *Good!* Rose thought. *Everything is ready. I hope I am ready, too. Please God help me to not make any mistakes today,* she prayed silently. Rose looked for her dad. He was seated next to Grandma. *I hope he isn't disappointed,* she thought. Dad had taken the day off from work to come and hear Rose recite her poem.

Rose heard the principal call her name. As Rose walked across the stage to the podium, Ruby and Christina walked behind her, and then stood beside her. Rose took a deep breath. Out of the corner of her eye, she could see Mrs. Rodriguez and the principal waving wildly at Ruby and Christina. Ruby and Christina didn't dare look over at them. They stared straight ahead with frozen smiles stretched across their faces. The three girls linked their hands, and Rose began to speak.

"Hope for Peace. An original poem by Camelia Huymahia." In unison, Rose, Ruby, and Christina said, "Our best Hijab-Ez friend!"

Christina and Ruby stood silently beside Rose as she recited Camelia's beautiful poem without one mistake. Rose knew she would be disqualified from the competition because she had not recited her own poem, but she didn't care. When she saw the beautiful smile that lit Camelia's face as she finished reciting her poem, Rose knew she had made the right PLAN.

Christina tugged on Rose's sleeve as parents, teachers, and students applauded. "Hurry up, Rose, the principal is coming!" Ruby was already headed towards the steps that lead to the main auditorium floor. Christina and Rose hurried after her. They walked quickly over to where their parents were standing to meet them. The girls got a big hug from their parents. Fahd and Abdul kept saying, "Subhanallah (Glory be to Him the Almighty)!"

Camelia hugged Rose, and, with tears of happiness shimmering in her eyes, she said quietly, "Thank you, dear friend." Rose's heart felt like it would burst from happiness when she heard Camelia's words!

A hush fell over the auditorium as the principal called out for everyone to be seated. "I have something important to say." Everyone sat down, and it got even quieter in the room.

"Thank you, Rose Allen, Ruby Nye, and Christina Gomez, for caring so much for your friend. You used a peaceful way to bring to our attention an error that was made. Our error caused a student in our school to be treated unfairly. I would like this student to come to the podium and recite her poem. Camelia Huymahia, please come to the podium and let the audience hear your beautiful poem again!"

Camelia's parents gave her a quick hug and gently pushed her forward.

The audience applauded loudly and stood as Camelia began to climb the steps to the stage podium. Camelia hesitated and turned to look back at her friends. With growing confidence and a song in her heart, she whispered just loud enough for her friends to hear, "This is the best PLAN you ever had!"

Camelia heard her friends whisper back, "Alhamduillah!" which means "All praise be to Allah!"

～

"Hurry up, Dad, or we're going to be late," called Rose as she waited impatiently at the front door.

"I'm almost ready." Dad walked into the kitchen smoothing down his unruly hair. "My, don't you look pretty!"

Rose grinned at her dad. She didn't often wear dresses, but today was a special occasion. Camelia's parents had invited Rose and her family to have lunch at the Casa Camelia Restaurant. The invitation said they wanted to thank Rose for helping Camelia get her poem read at the school's poetry contest.

"Camelia said that her father has a surprise for us. What do you think it could be?"

"When we get to the restaurant, I am sure we will find out," Dad replied patiently.

As Rose got into her Dad's truck, she looked over at Grandma's house. Abdul's car wasn't parked in the driveway. "I think Grandma, Grandpa, and the boys have already left," said Rose anxiously.

"Stop your worrying, Rose. We'll be there in twenty minutes." Dad smiled at his daughter and reminded her to fasten her seat belt.

Dad and Rose arrived at the Casa Camelia Restaurant and were greeted by Camelia's parents. Rose was amazed to see that the dining room was packed with many of Camelia's relatives, and Ruby and Christina's relatives and friends, and sitting with Camelia were Ruby and Christina.

Dad went to join Fahd, Abdul, and Grandpa at a table. Grandma went to sit with Camelia's mother, Judy, and Christina and Ruby's mothers.

After everyone got settled at a table, Mr. Huymahia, Camelia's father, asked for everyone's attention. "I have an announcement to make. The families of Camelia, Rose, Ruby, and Christina want to thank these young girls. Their loyalty, friendship, and acceptance of people of different races and religions are examples for each of us." Camelia's father walked over to the far wall and removed a blue cloth that was covering something hanging between two landscape pictures. Mounted on the wall were the four poems the Hijab-Ez had written. A plaque was mounted above the four, framed poems. Mr. Huymahia read the words on the plaque.

Hijab-Ez Friendship

Camelia Huymahia
Rose Allen
Ruby Nye
Christina Gomez

Rose, Camelia, Ruby, and Christina squealed their delight and hurried over to look at the framed poems and plaque. They raised their right hand with pinkie finger extended and said loudly, "Hijab-Ez! Friends forever!"

When the laughter and applause died down, Mr. Huymahia said, "We hope you will all enjoy your lunch."

That afternoon, Rose and her friends learned that winning a contest was nothing compared to the love and loyalty of family and friends.

Glossary

Glossary of Islamic Words and Definitions

A

Abaya—An outer covering Muslim women and girls wear over their clothes for modesty.

Abdul Muttalib—Muhammad's grandfather

Abdullah—Father of Muhammad (pbuh)

Abraham (ra)—Prophet of Allah

Abu Hurairah—Means "Cat Father" or "The Kitten Man"; a nickname given to a Muslim that memorized many sayings of the Prophet (Hadith). He asked God for knowledge that wouldn't be forgotten. He liked to play with cats and kittens and was very kind to them.

Abu Talib—Muhammad's uncle; Muhammad went to live with him when he was 10 years old after his grandfather died.

Abu Ummayah—An old and wise leader who lived in Mecca when Prophet Muhammad (pbuh) was a young man.

Abdur-Rahman—Means "Servant of the Merciful." He was a poor man who lived in Arabia and was known as Abdu-Shams. His name means "Servant of the Sun." He met Prophet Muhammad (pbuh) who changed his name. The Prophet (pbuh) didn't believe in worshipping idols. Some people worshipped the sun back in ancient days!

A'ishah (ra)—Wife of the Prophet (pbuh), young girl when she married him, ran races with the Prophet (pbuh), remembered many of the sayings of the Prophet (pbuh), many hadith are based on what she memorized and related about what the Prophet (pbuh) taught the Muslims, when she grew older the Muslims trusted her and asked her for advice.

Al-Ameen—Means "the Trustworthy One"; nickname for Prophet Muhammad (pbuh); he averted a war in Mecca because tribes were fighting about who would replace the black stone in the rebuilt Ka'bah.

Al-Fatihah—The Opening: the first Surah of the Qur'an and the first complete chapter taught to the Prophet.

Alhamdulillah—All praise be to Allah

Allah—God

Aminah—Mother of Prophet Muhammad (pbuh)

Angel Gabriel—The messenger of Allah to His Prophets

As-Sadiq—Means "Truthful One" (nickname of Muhammad)

Ash-Sham—Syria

B

Banu Hashim—Clan of the Quraish tribe

Banu Zahra—Tribe of Aminah in Mecca

Bahira—Christian monk living outside town of Basra, told Muhammad and his uncle, Abu Talib, that Muhammad was a Prophet

Birth mark—Shaped like an egg between Muhammad's shoulders; a sign he was a Prophet

Barakah—African servant of Aminah; helped to raise Muhammad after his mother died.

C

Cave of Hira—A small cave in a mountain outside of Mecca where the Angel Gabriel first spoke to the Prophet about the Qur'an. It took 23 years for the entire Qur'an to be revealed.

D

Dhuhr—Arabic name for noon prayer

E

Etiquette:
  - Muslims were taught by Prophet Muhammad (pbuh) to be neat and clean.

- Men should have beards and keep their fingernails clean and trimmed.
- Muslims should always have good manners. Prophet Muhammad (pbuh) said that the best of people have the best of manners.

F

Fatimah (ra)—Daughter of Prophet Muhammad, leader of all women Muslims in paradise
First Five People to Accept Islam:
    Khadijah – First believer and wife of the Prophet
    Zayd ibn Harith – Foster-son of the Prophet. He was once a slave.
    Ali – nine-year-old nephew of the Prophet
    Abu Bakr – Good friend, wealthy, head of his clan
    Barakah – Foster mother of the Prophet

H

Hadith—Hadith are sayings of the Prophet (pbuh) that Muslim scholars agree on with only a few differences. Scholars would check who reported the saying, and how many other people reported the same, or nearly the same, thing the Prophet (pbuh) said. Hadith are used to show what the Prophet said and did while he lived. This helps Muslims know how to live their lives as Muslims. Hadith help to explain what God means in the Qur'an.
Hafitha-ha, ya Allah—May Allah protect and preserve her
Hajar—Wife of Abraham (ra), mother of Isma'il and finder, by Allah's will, of the ZamZam well in Arabia.
Hajri-Aswad—Means "black stone." It is part of the first Ka'bah built by Prophet Abraham, sacred black stone.
Halima—Woman (tribe of Banu Sa'd) who took care of Muhammad for five years
Hijab—The covering a Muslim girl or woman chooses to wear that consists of a head covering and loose clothing to hide the shape of the body. The hijab scarf covers the hair entirely.

Usually only a Muslimah's face and hands are not covered. Some Muslim women choose to also cover their faces. There is also an "inner hijab." Inner Hijab is a Muslimah's modesty, willingness to obey God, and pride at being Muslim. Hijab is a state of mind, how you think and act.

Hijab-Ez—(pronounced hijab-ease) is a word that Rose made up to identify the group of Muslim and non-Muslim friends that joined together to support her hijab-wearing school friend, Camelia. A member of the Hijab-Ez is a girl who wears a head covering regardless of her religious beliefs.

I

'Iddah—Three month waiting period after a Muslimah gets divorced before she can get married again to another Muslim.

Isma'il—Son of Abraham (ra) and Hajar; Abraham's first-born son

Istikhara—A special du'a to Allah asking for help to make a decision.

J

Jibra'il—Arabic name for the Angel Gabriel

K

Ka'bah—Shrine that Abraham built to thank and honor Allah.

Khadijah—Muhammad's first wife; wealthy businesswoman; she was forty-years-old and Muhammad was twenty-five-years-old when they married.

M

Maghrib—Arabic name for the evening prayer

Masjid—A building where Muslims go to pray in congregation; usually has a dome and minaret.

Muhammad—Means "Highly Praised"; Prophet Muhammad (pbuh) was born in 570.
Miracle—Cloud hovering over the caravan Muhammad is traveling in proving, which proves he is a Prophet.

N

Nafisa—Khadijah's friend; she talked to Muhammad about marriage to Khadijah
Nasibah—Mother of Umarah, famous Muslimah warrior who fought many battles and defended the Prophet (pbuh) at the Battle of Uhud, one of the first 73 believers in Makkah who emigrated to Madinah
Nikkah—Marriage contract

P

Paradise—Heaven
Pledge—Prophet Muhammad (pbuh) was an orphan. He was always concerned for poor and oppressed people. He tried to help them. He took a pledge and kept this pledge all of his life.
Prophet Muhammad—Last Prophet and Messenger of Allah

R

Riba—paying interest on a loan; lottery, raffles and gambling are not permitted if you are a Muslim

S

Shepherd—Every Prophet has been a shepherd (takes care of animals—sheep)
Subhanallah—Glory be to Him the Almighty
Surah 96:1-5—Describes the Angel Gabriel ordering the Prophet (pbuh) to *READ*.

W

Waraqa—Blind uncle of Khadijah, he told her that Prophet Muhammad heard the same voice as Prophet Moses.

Wives of the Prophet (pbuh)—Khadijah, A'ishah, Zainab, Saudah, Hafsah, Umm Salamah, Zaynab, Juwairiyah, Umm Habibah, Safiyah and Maimunah

Y

Yathrib—City where Abdullah is buried (today it is called Medina)

Z

ZamZam Well—Allah caused water to come up from the sand and a well was formed in the earth below to hold water. The well is still used today and many people who drink the ZamZam water say that they have been healed from sickness.

Zaynab—Wife of the Prophet (pbuh) whose marriage contract was made by Allah.

A Special Note to Islamic Rose Readers

I hope you enjoyed reading the stories about Rose, her family, friends, and the Saudi police officers. I enjoy reading books, especially when the story is good and I can also learn something new. When I read a book that mentions a recipe that sounds like it might be delicious to eat or read a short description of a place I haven't traveled to, I want to try out the recipe or learn more about the interesting place.

This is why I have placed on my Islamic Rose Books website each *Recipe* mentioned in my books. I also created *Interesting Facts* which describe the fun places Rose, family and friends visit and there are many links to other websites that tell you more about these places.

To get your free *Recipes* or to read *Interesting Facts*, go to the Islamic Rose Books website at www.widad-lld.com, click on Books at the top of the screen, and then below each book cover you will see the link words **Recipes** or **Interesting Facts**. Just click either one and you will be able to print out the recipes or read the Interesting Facts. You will need Adobe Reader, which is a free software program to open these Links.

I hope you find the Interesting Facts fun to explore and maybe you will try one of the great recipes I have waiting for you. If you are a young reader, be sure you have an adult help you when you try the recipes. The original recipes were provided by Linda Kingston a sister friend of mine.

Don't forget to read other Islamic Rose Books: *The Visitors*, *Hijab-Ez Friends*, and *Saying Goodbye*. New books to the series will become available in the future. Thank you for reading *Stories*.

Linda Delgado

www.ingramcontent.com/pod-product-compliance
Lightning Source LLC
Chambersburg PA
CBHW032003040426
42448CB00006B/473